TELSA

THE TRUE STORY OF A DOG'S EXTRAORDINARY HEALING POWERS

TELSA

THE TRUE STORY OF A DOG'S EXTRAORDINARY HEALING POWERS

ROSEMARY STEPHENSON

FINDHORN PRESS

Edited by Jacqui Lewis
Cover design by Richard Crookes
Illustration (p.1) by Cheryl McAvoy, *www.tranquilartz.com*
Interior design by Damian Keenan
Printed and bound in the EU

Published by
Findhorn Press
117-121 High Street,
Forres IV36 1AB,
Scotland, UK

t +44 (0)1309 690582
f +44 (0)131 777 2711
e info@findhornpress.com
www.findhornpress.com

Contents

Dedication

I wish to dedicate this book to my dearest father, who has been my inspiration both as a philosopher and as a musician. His guidance and love has enriched my world a thousandfold and even more so from the spirit world. I am eternally grateful to him.

Acknowledgements

Grateful thanks to my dear son, Joe, for persuading me that to bring Telsa into our lives was the right thing to do when things were so challenging. Without you, my dearest Joe, this book would not be published!

Love and blessings also to Lewis who was a "second son" to me. He passed over to the other side on 12 September 2009. We will always remember you Lewis. I know you have been around with Telsa for this project.

Listed below are all my dear friends who have contributed in some way towards the contents of this little book.

Grateful thanks to Diana Cooper who has helped, pushed and spurred me on… keeping my motivation going to get this book published.

Grateful thanks to Edwin Courtenay, who channelled a message from St Francis, just after Telsa's passing, when I really needed that comfort and confirmation. For all his endless help and encouragement, together with Andrew, his partner, who always loved and welcomed Telsa into their home.

I am also grateful to Kate and Caroline for their endless support and Trudy for reminding me that I had choices in my life. Alice for proofreading together with Kate.

To Levi who has encouraged me so much to get this little book under way.

The list is endless.

Also for the warm-hearted generosity of all the people who have been touched in some way by Telsa and have contributed their love to this little book with their stories, Pippa, Barbara, Declan, Parveen, Julia, Caroline, Marcella, Glenys, Laura, Nadine, Sara and many more.

ODE TO TELSA
from Rosemary

True friends are so hard to find
When I forgot… she didn't mind
Always unconditional that was her trait
If I didn't have time, she would just wait
I loved her so much when she was here
Sometimes from a distance, not always near
But she understood how our relationship worked
She got on with it all and never shirked
So full of love, my dearest friend
Always there with a paw to lend
A wonderful healer and dedicated too
Telsa was there for me and you
She loved every minute of her occupation
And managed it all with dedication
My life as a healer has changed in some way
But I'm blessed she's with me every day

Doing the things you did before
Now I think you're doing even more
From the spirit world we can connect
For your love of healing and its effect

TELSA my angel, I miss you so much
But you are still with me, I feel your touch!

Foreword

This is the amazing true story of a boxer dog who had an extraordinary healing gift. The author's love for this remarkable animal shines from the pages as she describes how Telsa convinced even sceptics of the power of healing.

Rosemary explains how her boxer opened people's hearts and how even those who were terrified of dogs changed so completely that they started to love dogs instead.

This book contains many examples of how Telsa healed with the angels, and of Telsa holding the light, facilitating channelling experiences from group students.

Rosemary offers a number of special cases where Telsa gives healing, in which she could see the emerald-green light of Archangel Raphael being transferred from Telsa into the person being healed. Other people would also see or feel the phenomenon while it was happening.

Even after her death, Telsa's healing work continues; included here are many heartwarming stories of Telsa's spirit appearing to Rosemary and others, to comfort and help them in times of need.

If you love dogs and angels and are ready to open up your heart, then this is the book for you.

Diana Cooper

Introduction

In this book I share the story of Telsa's life, and of how she healed me, my son, my late husband and countless others during her lifetime. Even now, after her passing on 7 May 2009, three days before her eleventh birthday, she continues to work with and through me to heal and transform lives.

This is not just another book about animals' spiritual gifts. What Telsa gave to me to share with others was amazing: she showed me that our animals are eager to help us and all of humanity, and how to recognize their gifts and enable them to work with and for us.

I had used to think I lived alone, but it was not until Telsa had passed over that I realized what a massive part of my life she had been and how much she had lived with me.

Telsa was my eighth dog, if I include the dogs we had when I lived at home with my parents. I loved them all, but Telsa was a really special healing dog, who completely changed my life.

I have lived in close contact with animals as far back as I can remember, so this close affinity with animals was developed at an early age. As I was born and spent my childhood on a farm, I was always in the company of pigs, cows, sheep, horses, hens, dogs, cats, rabbits and more.

I was born at Birch Tree Farm in Cheshire, where we had many animals. We had a few adult pigs and there was always one sow or another giving birth to piglets, so it was a regular occurrence in our house to be feeding baby piglets with a bottle wrapped up in a blanket. There was always the runt, which was the weakest one, who got pushed to one side and would die if we didn't intervene.

There were three of us children, myself and my two sisters, Madeline and Isabel, and we all desperately wanted to be the one to feed the baby piglets, so my father used to organize a rota system to keep the peace!

I remember the dog I had the most affinity with when I was young. He was a golden Staffordshire bull terrier, named Spot the singing dog. Spot was such a softy and so friendly to humans, but he stood no nonsense from other dogs and would never allow another dog near our house. Only protecting his own, I suppose!

I always loved hens; there is something about them that I find endearing. When I was in my late twenties and living close to the sea in Morecambe Bay, I decided I would like to have six hens and so went to buy a henhouse. There was a brook running through the bottom of the garden that was perfect for them. I made a run for them and with the henhouse and the water they had a perfect setting. I became very close to the hens, who liked to fly over the fence and wander about in the garden and into the house. There was one particular hen, named Clara, who was bossier than the others and always wanted her own way. She demanded attention in the mornings. She would sit on the fence close to the kitchen window, waiting for me to get up. When she saw me she would peck at the window until I opened the door and gave her something to eat. In the end, especially if I was late for work, I would have to crawl along the kitchen floor and reach up to put the kettle on, and then crawl back to the bathroom so that she couldn't see me. I had a beagle at this time called Freddie, and. when I put his food outside Clara would fly at him and peck him and not let him have his food. She was like a guard dog and her ways made me very fond of her, but one sad day she met her fate and a fox claimed her life – I am sure not without a battle on her part. The only being who seemed happy that day was Freddie the dog, who could at last eat his food in peace!

Many years later my husband, our young son Joe and I moved to a smallholding and I was immediately transported back to my childhood, surrounded as it had been with animals.

We had ducks, hens, geese, pheasants, working dogs and our special friend Lisa the lamb. We adopted Lisa as a baby when her mother rejected her, and she became the most prominent pet in this household and had her own field and wooden house.

Joe and I shared her bottle-feeding, which had to be done a few times a day. As she grew older and had more contact with us, she became more and more "human". No one messed with Lisa or could fail to notice that she was around: she would kick her bowl when she was hungry and rattle the gate for water or if she wanted to go for a walk in the fields on her lead. Joe would always get pulled off his feet while holding on to her lead; we were never sure who was taking whom for a walk! He and his friends used to tease her and she would headbutt them.

It was always a difficult time when Lisa was due back at the local farm for shearing. She would not allow any of the men to put her into the Land Rover, only myself or Joe. She would fight and headbutt everyone else. What a character she was.

I remember the first Bonfire Night after Lisa had arrived with us. We had invited some of Joe's friends and their mums over and we had an old caravan that had an oven, tables and chairs, and was ideal for this sort of gathering. The only thing we hadn't taken into consideration was Lisa.

We started the bonfire and the fireworks and Lisa went crazy, crying and running back and forth. We had temporarily forgotten that she might be disturbed by the fireworks. I spent most of the evening cuddled up to Lisa in her house until the fireworks had finished. I'm sure this created a special bonding friendship between us.

She would escape to the vegetable plot and gorge on all those lovely meals on tap – too much to resist! We decided to have some hens again, and put the henhouse in Lisa's field. She became the guard dog for the hens and for our house too. No fox, nor even any other human being come to that, would have dared to confront her.

When we eventually left West Farm because of separation and divorce, my friends took Lisa to live at their farm, sharing a field with their goat Rosie. It was love at first sight and they lived happily together for the rest of their days.

I had been married to a very charismatic, dynamic businessman who was the father of my son Joe. Unfortunately alcohol had begun to play too great a part in my husband's life and the problems this brought sapped my confidence and began to affect Joe. I began to despair of our marriage. To help ease our situation I took Joe and his friends, especially his best friend Lewis, on caravan holidays as often as we could to escape from it all.

As a child I had been weaned on music, but over the previous five years had not touched a musical instrument or sung a note. Despite our situation, I managed to get myself back into the music that I had loved so much. Here I could escape from my growing fear and anger of my husband: it was my saving grace. I decided to further my music and attended Newcastle College. It was wonderful to be singing and playing once more. I didn't realize at this time that the music and the singing were going to be my healing therapy, but they were, and this was the beginning of my road to recovery.

I was beginning to grow in confidence more and more, which did not help the household situation. My husband was losing control over me and that didn't work for him. The day came when I would put up with no more.

I arranged for a van to take my belongings to my house in Walton Park, which I had bought previously with my inheritance, and quickly moved out with Joe.

I could now see a way of getting my life back together. I could see a pathway before me; although it was not going to be easy it was clearly there.

Joe, who was nine years old now, and I, moved into the small house for a while until I could get back to work at Wansbeck General Hospital in Northumberland. His father decided not to keep the animals from the smallholding and handed them all over to us. What was already a small house became even smaller as we tried to find room for all the animals: four tortoises, a chinchilla and two black Labradors.

It was a tight squeeze in our new home but we managed for a while. Eventually, though, we did have to rehouse most of the animals. I knew Joe needed a friend while we were going through our separation and divorce and that to lose all his animal friends was difficult for him, but I also knew that this would have to be the way until we were settled.

Joe and I then moved into a lovely house not too far from his father so he could visit when he liked. This was the start of a new life for me. I renovated the house and we enjoyed the peace and quiet for as long as it was going to last.

Joe eventually persuaded me that I should at least consider having another dog. Enter Telsa, who turned us all upside down but changed our lives in a wonderful way forever.

In spite of all the unhappy times, I am thankful that Joe's father came into my life to give me all my many challenges and lessons. I am happy to say that he eventually managed to turn himself around and learned some of these lessons too. What was really amazing was that after all those huge challenges we became very close friends in the last three years before he passed over in March 2005. It seemed we had come full circle. I am so grateful for that experience.

PART I

A Mischievous
Puppy

Telsa Comes into Our Lives

It was now 1998. Joe, my son, was fifteen. Although we were very settled in our new home, not surprisingly Joe was still very disturbed by the break-up of his family home and as a result his schoolwork was suffering. Joe desperately wanted another dog as he had lost both of his dogs after we left our family home. They were two black Labradors, which Joe was very close to. He had also had a chinchilla, a lamb, tortoises and hens, all of which were a large part of his life.

I was feeling that Joe's schoolwork and the fact that he wasn't happy in his present school was a more important issue than our old pets at this point. Rather than taking on another puppy in the middle of all this chaos, I managed to persuade him to put it on hold, thinking that maybe he would get over his longing for another dog. We both felt that we should try to find another school for him, and it was going to be hard work as he was to sit his GCSE exams the following year; this was a critical time for him.

I decided to approach the colleges around Tynemouth and Newcastle to see if they would accept him for his last year. Two of the heads were sympathetic but said they couldn't, as the education authorities would not allow it. There was one more chance. I prayed to the angels, my father and anyone else who would listen.

I made a final attempt to meet with the head of North Tyneside College. I was now desperate.

The head was very sympathetic but again he didn't hold out much hope of being able to take Joe in for his final year. He agreed to try for us, though. The wait for that decision seemed to go on forever, but I didn't give up hope and kept on praying to the angels.

At last, I received a phone invitation to meet up with the head of the College again.

He told me the best news ever – he said this was the first time that the education authorities had ever allowed this to happen, but that they were willing to give us a chance. WOW. "Thank God!" I shouted. I jumped up and hugged this man who I believed had been guided to help us.

It is so wonderful how amazing things do happen and how people are put in front of us when we really need and ask for help. I have since realized that this has happened to me many times during my lifetime.

We sat together and sorted a timetable for Joe's part-time attendance so that he could fit in with the subjects the College were offering.

Joe was now beginning to feel much happier and was able to focus more on his work. He hadn't forgotten about the puppy idea, though, and began scouring the Internet for breeders of boxer puppies. I just couldn't imagine how we would deal with a puppy at this moment, and tried to persuade him it was not the best time to do this. He kept looking, though, and trying to win me over. He eventually found a breeder not too far away from us and showed me the pictures of the puppies and parents. I had to be thankful that for the first time in ages Joe had positive thoughts in his life, so I eventually gave in (and also the puppies looked so gorgeous!). At last things in our lives seemed to be coming together and I knew we were receiving help to move us both further on to this positive pathway.

I agreed to ring the breeder to arrange a time for us to visit the puppies. All the pups had been sold but they were able to offer one to us as the original new owner's circumstances had changed.

It was 12 August 1998 when Joe and I went to look at Telsa. I remember because we could hear the game shooters on the moors as we approached the breeder's house. We were so excited about meeting this puppy that we had temporarily forgotten about those poor pheasants being shot. It made us both think of the time when we had lived in the family smallholding and Joe's father had bred pheasants for the shooters. We had a caravan in the field for the boys to camp out in, but it came in very handy in another way as shooting time approached; Joe and I lined it with straw and gathered and hid as many of the pheasants as we could. We fed the pheasants until the shooters had finished and gone away, and then we set them free.

We continued travelling across the moors, the guns in the distance, and finally arrived excitedly at the farm in Middleton-in-Teesdale.

It was a real dog-loving home and the owners were lovely people. Their farmhouse felt very "lived-in" and the dogs and puppies were very happy. The adult dogs, living in large kennels outside, were all show dogs and the farm had recently won an award at Crufts for best boxer.

When we and the dogs were introduced, in bounded the adult ones first of all; these were all Telsa's relatives, so we were under no illusions about what type of dog Telsa would grow up to be – we could see what her family was like. The dogs were all very excited, jumping all over us. Then three adorable brindle puppies raced in to meet us. We didn't know at this point which one was Telsa, but they were all gorgeous. Joe lay on the living-room floor with these puppies scrambling all over him and he was loving every minute of it. Joe then got up and sat on a chair and one of the puppies started trying to climb on to his knee. When the breeders told us that this was the puppy on offer, we just looked at each other, broke into huge smiles and knew that this was the right thing to do. Telsa had chosen Joe, that was for sure. How fantastic! That was it: the deal was done.

We put Telsa in the car, feeling excited. To see Joe's face as he held her in his arms in the car was priceless and I knew that this new puppy was absolutely right for us. No amount of money could have bettered how we felt that day. Telsa snuggled in to Joe, shivering for a while, but soon settled down. I am sure she was wondering where we were taking her, away from all her brothers and sisters.

We arrived home and the reality began to set in for me. How was I going to manage to hold down my job at the hospital as well as keeping an eye on Joe at college and a new puppy in the house? With the help of a few good friends we managed to juggle all the balls and keep most of them, at least, in the air!

A friend, Michelle, agreed to come to clean our house and look after Telsa for two mornings a week while I was at work and Joe at college.

I managed to persuade my boss to allow me to do two long days at work so I could spend the rest of the week at home. Joe looked after Telsa when he wasn't at college and between us we seemed to be managing.

Telsa was a typical boxer puppy – full of life and so loving. Just what we had needed. It was very hard work but Joe pulled his weight and looked after Telsa as much as his college timetable and work would allow him. To see the two of them together was like a gift from heaven!

As part of this new adventure we bought an indoor puppy cage/ kennel with a cosy sheepskin rug for Telsa to sleep in, a dog flap and toys for her. Joe was so much happier now. What joy this puppy had brought into our lives already! She was a handful, but it didn't seem to matter; overall this beautiful, bouncy, loving boxer had changed our lives for the better. We had to go through all the usual puppy antics: Telsa chewed everything in sight. The toilet rolls were always being unravelled halfway down the stairs. Shoes were always missing and usually to be found at the bottom of the garden. I remember she chewed my new camera. Nothing was sacred to her. This lasted until she was about a year old; it seemed that her toys were not nearly as exciting as an old smelly shoe or a sock. She was so adorable though that whatever she did we forgave her.

About two years later I began to realize that I was consciously moving towards a more spiritual pathway. It was an accident that confirmed this to me. I was now working at the RVI Hospital in Newcastle and had arranged to meet a friend, Jan, for lunch. I was rushing around as usual and slipped on a piece of fruit as I was entering a nearby café. The manager sent for an ambulance even though the hospital was just up the road. I knew most of the doctors and nurses in the A & E department there, so you can imagine the stick I received. I had minor injuries but had to take a few weeks off, and it was during this time that I realized I had to change my life. It was another wake-up call: yes, another one. There had been so many times, when I think back, that I ignored these calls, but this time I was going to take notice.

I had recently seen a clairvoyant, Trudy, who had reminded me that I had choices in my life, and I knew that now was the time to put them into action.

I was still having problems with Joe's father even though we were no longer living in the same house. I decided that living in

Newcastle wasn't working for me, and I spoke to Joe, told him I wanted to go back to live in Cheshire and asked if he would be happy to come with me. I was feeling very drawn to go back to my roots and where I had grown up with my father, who had been so close to me. I knew I couldn't be totally free while I lived so near to my ex-husband.

I had lost my father in 1989. I had recently had a major operation in Newcastle and my father was admitted to hospital in Cheshire for tests. I had packed my case for the right time to visit him, but alas, it was not meant to be. He passed suddenly and unexpectedly. I was devastated and full of anger and guilt. I had been denied the chance to say goodbye to the most important man in my life.

I was feeling now that getting back into my music was what my father would have wanted me to do. He had been a musician, singer and choirmaster and I had worked with him from my very early childhood. The connection between us was very strong and we'd loved singing and playing music together. Getting seriously back into music really helped me to connect to him and accept that he had passed away.

Some years later, in 2007, I experienced guidance, as a presence, from my father. He appeared to me surrounded by a beautiful golden light, telling me that he had had to leave suddenly so that I would have a strong desire to contact him so much once he was in spirit. He was very proud of the work I was doing with my music and the angels.

This was wonderful confirmation to me and made a lot of sense of all that had been happening.

Telsa's
Personality

There was no denying that Telsa as she was growing up was a character, a very lively, full-of-life puppy. She had a beautiful gentle expression and nature and, until she started to fill out at two years old, long spindly legs. She loved retrieving sticks, balls and especially Frisbees. She never tired of these games, right up to her passing at eleven years old. Right from the beginning of her life with us there was no doubt that she was making her presence felt in our household.

Joe loved taking her everywhere with him on walks and playing with her. She loved him and wanted to be with him all the time. It seemed, at that time anyway, that she was definitely Joe's dog.

This particular day Joe had taken Telsa out for a walk along the hilly coastline of Tynemouth, where we lived. There were green hills sloping down to the cliff edge and the sea and, close by, the old remains of the monastery, Tynemouth Priory. It was a spectacular place for walking. Joe was meeting a couple of friends, who loved Telsa. Just as well, as the two of them were inseparable by now.

She was very playful and boisterous. The boys and Telsa were all running around with a ball when Telsa spotted a small rabbit running over the hills and immediately went into chase mode. Joe called her but she had her focus on the rabbit and ran until she disappeared over the hill. Joe, frantically chasing after her, realized she had disappeared over the cliff edge. He called out to her again and she began to whimper. She had fallen over the edge but had managed to land on a ledge. Joe was terrified that she would try to move and fall even further, so he scrambled down to reach her. She was in shock and stayed still until Joe grasped her and carried her back to safety. He rushed home in a panic with Telsa in his arms and we immediately took her to the vet, who treated her for shock and bruising.

Telsa was still with us. Little did I know that this was to be just the first of many scrapes she would get herself into.

One day I arrived home from work and called to Telsa. I thought it unusual that she didn't greet me as she had full view of the front of the house from the landing window, which was her lookout post. I looked round, then went upstairs, and there she was on my bed – with one of our tortoises. She was wrestling with it. The poor thing must have had the shock of its life. I think she thought it was a live bone. I quickly grabbed the tortoise, fearing for its life, and knew that there was not enough room at our home for the four tortoises and Telsa. Although we were reluctant, we had to rehome them immediately and we found a family down the road who were absolutely delighted to take them.

One afternoon a few weeks later, Joe had decided to go to visit his best friend Lewis, who lived across the busy main road. He asked me to keep an eye on Telsa and, although I was staying at home, I locked the front and back doors as Telsa was a great escape artist. Off Joe went.

What I hadn't realized was that the "up-and-over" garage door was open, as was the door from the kitchen leading through to the garage. Before I could reach the door, Telsa shot off through the garage like an Olympic athlete. It was too late, and she was much too fast for me to catch her. She sprinted down our road and I knew she just wanted to get to Joe – and would have to run over the main road to do so. Joe, standing waiting at Lewis's door, was horrified to hear the screech of brakes and see Telsa being tossed into the air by a fast-moving car. It all happened so quickly. I could hear Joe screaming and shouting as he ran back to our house with Telsa in his arms.

Off to the emergency vet we went again. This was becoming a frightening habit. The vet checked her over and miraculously she had survived with just bruising, shock and a broken claw. Another miracle. We were so thankful that our dear beloved friend had been spared once again, although we were not to know the reason why until much later.

By this time I had realized that Telsa was not going to be one of those quiet, stay-at-home dogs. Joe and I had our hands full and we knew it. The following day my first job was to get her insured – we knew we had an unpredictable future ahead of us.

We had so much fun with Telsa though. I had gone out for a couple of hours to do some shopping and left her at home, as she had her dog flap to get in and out of the house and garden whenever she liked. I closed all the downstairs rooms and upstairs bedrooms so she had the run of the large kitchen, hall and landing and the garden.

When I arrived back home I realized that I had locked myself out; I had pulled the front door closed and left the key inside. Telsa was jumping up at the window wondering why I wasn't coming into the house. I would have to get to her, but Joe was out at college and I could only do that by climbing over the garage and into the back garden where she could meet me. I climbed over the garage, hoping the neighbours wouldn't see me and wonder what was going on. Telsa was delighted to see me when I jumped down into the garden, and ran into the house through the dog flap – expecting me to follow her, I'm sure. I realized that maybe this was actually a good idea; there was no other way I was going to get into the house for the few hours until Joe came home. Just as well I was a bit slimmer in those days too!

I put my head through the flap and Telsa immediately began to lick my face and climb over my head. She thought we were playing a game and wouldn't leave me alone. I forced one arm through and then the other and pushed hard to get the rest of my body through. I was exhausted as Telsa was still jumping on me and licking me. Suddenly I had another big realization: Telsa was so happy about me coming in through the dog flap – if she was as pleased to see anyone else coming in that way, she probably wasn't going to be the best burglar deterrent in town!

Healing Other Dogs

By now, at about eighteen months old, Telsa was beginning to settle down. Well, as settled down as a boxer was ever going to be.

Things had also become more peaceful with Joe's father and he was visiting occasionally, with his dog Chris the black Labrador.

Chris kept herself to herself and did not like to play with other dogs. She was an excellent working dog, a retriever, so the idea of having other dogs as friends had never entered the equation. She tolerated them well, but that was all. She only loved humans and wanted all the attention she could get, not wanting to share that attention with any other dog.

Telsa would jump back and forth at Chris to make her play but Chris didn't want to know. Telsa persevered time and time again, trying to get her to play. She would not take "no" for an answer, even with all the growling and snapping she received from Chris.

At last Chris gave in and for the first time in her life began to play with another dog. Life had been just a competition with other dogs as far as she was concerned, but she began to really enjoy this very new pastime and she and Telsa became the best of friends. Chris had found a new dimension to her life, which I doubt she would ever have found without Telsa's help and persistence.

On a spiritual level, I feel Telsa had opened Chris's heart.

While living in Tynemouth, Joe and I would go to Cheshire from time to time to visit my family. My sister Isabel had a large Rott-weiler named Beth who definitely did not like other dogs at all and certainly didn't want to play. Like Chris, she only liked humans and felt that other dogs were a threat to her relationship with them.

I told my sister about Telsa and Chris becoming the best of friends and that I was sure it would be good for Beth and Telsa to get together. We decided to just leave them to get on with it. Beth was not too happy at first and didn't really want to play but Telsa just persevered. She really made us laugh with her antics as we now knew how she worked and how she would break down the other dog's defences. She would literally box Beth with her paw, which is a well-known characteristic of boxer dogs.

Again, after a couple of visits Telsa won Beth over and from then on, just like her and Chris, they were the best of friends.

We began to see a pattern emerging. Telsa was so determined to play that the other dogs just had to give in. She would persevere and persevere until she had opened other dog's hearts – as well as human hearts.

Similar things would happen when we were walking in the fields. Telsa was so friendly that I trusted her and used to let her off the lead; she loved the freedom to approach the dogs we met along the way. Some dogs were friendly to and some were not. I suppose they are just the same as humans, who get on with some people but find it more difficult to get on with others.

This particular day Telsa and I were walking in the field next to our house when we saw in the distance a large black long-haired dog with his owner. Benny was the dog's name and he was a cross between a terrier and a German Shepherd. This dog was notorious for not liking people and, even more, other dogs. His owner, Jim, would shout out to everyone to put their dog on the lead because he was fearful of what might happen.

Most people thought that Benny's owner was an angry man with an angry dog but I realized that he was frightened and panicking and so, inevitably, was his dog. Jim was afraid of what might happen and I really felt for him. It must have been difficult enough for Jim to keep coming out day after day and walking Benny as he was advancing in years and I am sure he was worried that Benny would pull him down and escape. As time went by I realized more and more what a hard time Jim was having with his dog; no wonder it was making him stressed and therefore angry. He was fearful of the reception he would get from other dog owners, and I am sure that didn't help with Benny's behaviour; as we know, our animals pick up on our energy very easily, much more easily than humans do. If we are happy then our animals are happy. If we are stressed they feel it immediately and therefore go into protective mode for their owner.

Telsa, being Telsa, loved a challenge. This was the biggest challenge we had faced so far, though, and I wasn't sure that I was keen to go along with it. As it turned out, I had no choice. I usually let Telsa off the lead in the field so she could enjoy a good run and the freedom, but when this particular dog was around I always kept her on the lead. I had no idea that this was going to be the day that I lost control of that. Unexpectedly, Telsa decided to tug and managed to slip her head from her collar and escape. She went straight for Benny, bounding up to this very unhappy, angry dog. Benny dived at Telsa, pulling Jim over as we had always feared, and his dog got away. I called to Telsa, to no avail, and just stood there helplessly as she carried on running. I hadn't got a clue what would happen next.

Jim was very shaken so I went over to help him up. He was panicking and angry with me because of Telsa's action. I tried to ignore his anger and just asked him if he was OK and sat him on the grass. By the time we looked over at the two dogs, Telsa had worked her magic and quietened Benny down and they were lying side by side. Telsa being her usual self had been persistent in trying to make Benny play with her. I was too far away from them to do anything about it. I think the angry dog was so exhausted by Telsa that in the end he just lay down, with her beside him licking him and showing him affection.

Jim could not believe his eyes. He had rescued Benny from the dog shelter seven years previously and he told me that Benny had always been an angry dog. I could see in Jim's eyes that he was melting towards Telsa and also towards his own dog. We walked over to the dogs, put them on their leads and walked alongside them in the field. Things were really changing.

I suggested we let them off the leads and they ran off and played together. It was wonderful to see them having such a lovely time. Even greater was the lovely smile on the old man's face, a smile I was seeing for the first time.

Benny and his owner's lives changed dramatically after this incident. Jim began to enjoy walking his dog and Telsa enjoyed playing with them both. Benny slowly began to tolerate other dogs with Telsa's encouragement and company, and everyone noticed a big change in both the dog and his owner.

I didn't really understand at the time what was happening, but I soon began to realize that Telsa was doing amazing things and that she was a special dog, a mediator for other dogs, and that I just had to hang on to my hat and enjoy the ride while it all went on.

Little did I know what was to happen over the next few years or where this would take both of us.

All our pets are special if we allow them to be and understand how sensitive they are. How unconditional too. They usually come to us at a time when we need them most, and they have amazing gifts to bring with them if we take the time to notice and recognize them. We have to remember that our animals are naturally more tuned in to energies than humans; they pick up our thoughts and feelings immediately and respond to them. If only they could speak the same language as us – the guidance they could share would be amazing. If we take the time, though, we can sit and tune in telepathically with our dogs and get to know their needs. They certainly know our needs, if we will only listen to them and take notice of their behaviour when they are trying to help us or tell us something.

Telsa in the Caravan

A little while later, in 2002 when I had moved to Cheshire, I decided to look for a workshop or a course to help me connect with the angels. As I had been reading Diana Cooper's books, *The Power of Inner Peace* and *A Little Light on Ascension*, I decided I would like to do a workshop with this lady. I was particularly drawn to the teacher-training course in Bergerac, France. I wasn't sure how I would be able to do this as I hadn't even been to an angel workshop at this point, but I decided to send for the brochure and worry about it later. It all seemed so out of reach but still I couldn't get it out of my head. Then, a few days later, a funny thing happened. Trudy, the clairvoyant, rang me to see how I was. We didn't know each other very well at this time and I was pleasantly surprised that she had rung. She told me someone had mentioned this teacher-training course in France but she wasn't sure if she should go because she didn't like flying and thought she would be homesick. I just had a funny feeling that we were both looking at the same course. I asked her if it was the Diana Cooper course and she said it was! We were both so surprised that we were looking at the same course and wondering whether to do it. I said she should do it but didn't think I was ready. Immediately a picture jumped off the wall behind me; the hanger and nail were still in place, so they hadn't just given way. It fell and smashed as it landed on my head and shoulder. I shouted out as it was so painful, and dropped the telephone. When I managed to get myself together I realized that the painting was of Notre Dame in Paris … that had to be the sign I had been waiting for! I made up my mind there and then and so did Trudy. It is amazing the lengths the angels will go to get us to where we are meant to be. If we are resisting then we have to suffer the consequences, falling pictures or whatever else they may be.

When I had thought about it later my logical head came in again and decided I would like to see what Diana was like before I went on the course. I arranged to attend an evening talk in Stourbridge just a few weeks before the course in France began. I don't know why I went to this talk. I think it might have been to check whether I would be ready and prepared for this trip. The talk was excellent and to my surprise I felt that I was ready for the course.

When I went to my room that night in the sixteenth-century hotel, plenty of things started to happen involving spirit energies from the past and stuck souls, and I was awake for most of the night; these mischievous souls had decided to prevent me having a good night's sleep. There were a few spirit beings there who had decided to take advantage of me to help them to the light.

First there was a middle-aged gentleman in clothing suggesting the 1600s, who said he had been murdered in this building. He had been living between the Earth plane and the spiritual astral plane and was ready to go to the light now, but needed help.

I called to Archangel Michael for protection, Archangel Sandalphon to keep me grounded to the Earth and the Gold Ray of Christ, which also offers powerful protection. I asked the angels for a pillar of white light and asked the gentleman to stand in it so the angels could take him to the light if he was willing. He was willing: off he went, waving as he disappeared.

There was also a little girl of about six years old, dressed in a long white Victorian nightgown and nightcap, who had been playing and had fallen to her death through the bedroom window.

I also encountered a family from the time of the Second World War who had all died in a fire in the house.

With the angels, I helped all these spirits to go to the light, but it left me very tired and I overslept and missed my alarm call in the morning. I rushed downstairs late, thinking that I had missed breakfast.

It was very quiet as I arrived at reception. The receptionist said that most of the guests had gone to work by now so I would have the very large breakfast room to myself. There was plenty of choice of where to sit but I felt that there was someone else in the room even before I had looked. My goodness – it was Diana Cooper! And she asked me to join her for breakfast. Blimey, I thought. I couldn't believe this and I knew I couldn't get out of it now. I had to face it.

Being tired after my disturbed night was making me feel less positive and raising doubts in me again. Well, I thought, at least I will know now. She will tell me if I am not ready for the intensive teacher-training course in France, so I might as well just get on with it.

Diana asked me if I was working with the angels and I said I would love to be. I told her I had applied for her course in France. After we had talked and finished breakfast Diana said she would see me in three weeks in France.

Brilliant, I thought, that was my confirmation to do it. I must go for it now.

This was another synchronicity for me. Just as I was feeling that maybe I wouldn't be ready for this course the angels made me late so that Diana and I would have to meet up, after all the other guests had left the breakfast room, to dispel my fears. This was a major turning point in my life.

A few weeks later, in March 2003, Trudy and I met in Newcastle and travelled to France together. The course was life-changing and I came back a different person. I felt I had been fast-tracking for three weeks, as if to make up for lost time. I went into the course feeling quite inadequate and came out feeling that the world was my oyster. I certainly had my light put on over those special three weeks. So much information! Absolutely life-changing. I truly thank the angels and Diana for that experience. There were so many things to put into practice. All those wake-up calls I had ignored in the past were now so obvious to me.

When I arrived home I went to collect Telsa from my friend Lynn, who had a smallholding way out in the country in south Cheshire. She had an Alsatian called Zak, who, again after some coaxing, eventually gave in to Telsa's antics and friendly advances. This worked out really well for Telsa – as a result of this friendship, she was allowed in the house, the only dog that was, to sleep with Zak. I think she was much wiser than I had realized. She knew how to make life easier for herself too!

I decided after collecting Telsa that we would go straight up to our caravan, which was sited in Knaresborough, North Yorkshire. This part of the world has always been a favourite place of mine. It all seems so familiar and feels very special to me. My caravan was a small tourer and was very cosy and compact. Telsa and I both loved it there. I began to notice as the evening went on that Telsa was watching me more carefully than she usually did, looking around me, moving her head from side to side as though she were recognizing someone. I felt that she was seeing spirit beings or angels in the caravan. I knew I felt very different since my course in France, but Telsa had obviously noticed too. I also began to see a lot of light around her and wondered then if maybe she had been sent to me to help me with the healing work I was to do in the future.

My caravan was sited in a beautiful setting and the site owners were very helpful and friendly to Telsa and me and interested in the spirit world and what we were doing. Peter, the groundsman, had told me they were going to get some peacock eggs to breed them, which apparently was not so easy to do.

Before very long there were a few peacocks wandering around and it was amazing how quickly they multiplied. They decided to roost in a very tall tree next to our caravan, which was absolutely marvellous, despite the noise they made before retiring.

Telsa and I would watch them as they flew high up into the tree and settled for the night, managing to balance on the branches. It was amazing how they managed to stay on their perches while they were sleeping. We both loved watching this evening ritual, and in the morning the peacocks would wander up to the caravan and "shout" for food.

I have had a fascination with peacocks for as long as I can remember, so it was a joy to be surrounded by these beautiful creatures. Telsa was quite used to having them around and they seemed to be oblivious to her too. Peacock feathers were in abundance and my house and caravans were filled with them.

Within a few months I had begun to teach angel healing courses with Declan, a friend I had met on the teacher-training course in France. I was also teaching sound and music therapies, as music was my first love and I was very keen to use my passion for helping people. Declan and I had agreed to start our first weekly evening healing groups in Manchester but as it turned out, I was really thrown in at the deep end, as Declan had to drop out of teaching some of the courses. He had done his job in getting me started, though, and I thank him for that. I started to attune willing participants to angelic reiki healing. I taught most of these classes from my home or my larger caravan in Cheshire. Telsa was always with me and I had begun to notice how she loved the meditations and music and also my very special crystal singing bowls, which I used as a musical instrument to accompany the meditations.

I would ask the members of our group to close their eyes and relax for the meditation and Telsa would roll over on her side, with a big sigh, ready to take part with the others. The members of the group would laugh and smile at her as she joined in with whatever we were doing, just like a human.

Another event showed me Telsa's powerful ability to link with spirit.

Diana and I were at my large static caravan in Cheshire, by the river and surrounded by trees and fields. This caravan was really like another home to me. We were talking about the large and very successful angel event the previous day at Trentham Gardens in Stoke-on-Trent. We began talking about the masters and the angels, and all of a sudden I felt a massive energy come in and saw a large ball of white misty energy start to build up around Telsa, getting larger and larger. I saw the Masters of Light enter our space, all standing in a row. They had come to thank us for putting on the event and celebrate how successful for the Light it had been. I know Telsa played a massive part in that channelling by holding the light for us.

This seemed to be a very special healing partnership, I thought, and Telsa continued to exceed all my expectations.

PART II

Telsa Develops as a Healer

Telsa's First Healings

After some years of turbulence I managed to make friends again with my ex-husband, with the help of Archangel Michael and Telsa.

My son Joe was feeling unsettled in Cheshire as all his friends were still in Newcastle. He had decided to move back there to be with his greatest friend Lewis. They were inseparable and were more like twins than friends, with a very close connection. Joe would travel up and down the country to be with me and then travel back to Tynemouth, near Newcastle, to be with his father and friends.

Joe's father was very angry with me for moving away and made it difficult for me to meet up with Joe, which is why, as mentioned in the previous chapter, I had bought another caravan and sited it in Knaresborough, Yorkshire. This made it easier for me to get to Newcastle with Telsa, so we could both keep in better touch with Joe.

At home one evening, I was feeling really upset. Joe's father would not allow me to speak to Joe on the phone. I was sure he also wasn't telling Joe when I tried to ring. It was becoming very difficult to keep in contact with Joe unless he rang me.

I went to bed very upset that evening, and asked the angels what I should do. How could I make things better and make it easier for me and Joe to see each other? I was at my wits' end.

At about 5 a.m. in the morning I was awakened by a white light surrounded by a brilliant blue glow. I heard a voice and sat bolt upright in bed: the voice said to me "You have to make friends with him." How was I going to do that? I thought. Then I realized that it was Archangel Michael who was speaking to me and that he was going to give me the strength, courage and protection I needed to do this. I instantly began to feel strength and courage welling up in me and knew I had to do it.

I had always been in fear of my husband when he had been drinking. He was a very tall, large-framed man who was very intimidating and not easy to deal with. I decided though that, with the help of the angels, I was going to give this a try.

I arranged to meet Joe in Newcastle. Telsa was so excited; she always knew when she was going to see Joe.

Telsa and I travelled up in the car, stayed overnight in the caravan then travelled up to Newcastle the following morning. I was feeling very positive and knew something good was about to happen, although what it was, I didn't know. We went out for a meal and took Telsa for a walk along the beach. It was so good to see them together again. Joe missed her so much and she missed him too. It was a very difficult situation for all of us.

I asked Joe if it would be easier for him if I could be friends with his dad and he said of course, but how was I ever going to do that?

We had a plan: that was to go back into his house and I would arrive later, knock at the door and hopefully speak to his dad.

I dropped Joe off and, later on, summoned the courage to knock at the door, knowing Archangel Michael was with me.

Joe came to the door and I heard him telling his father that I wanted to speak to him. His father came to the door. He looked very intimidating, with hands on his hips, asking what I wanted. I told him that I would like us to make friends so that it would be easier for Joe to see both of us and that life was far too short to be angry and hurt.

He asked me if I had anything else to say, but I had said everything I wanted to. He slammed the door shut and left me standing in the rain.

Previously I would have stood and cried and then just got back into the car and driven away. But this time something or someone was making me go back again. It was definitely Archangel Michael spurring me on, I knew it. This time I took Telsa out of the car and knocked at the door again. Joe opened the door, surprised to see me back again.

This time I went into the hallway and shut the door behind me with Telsa on her lead sitting right beside me. When Joe's father came out, I told him that I was not going anywhere this time until he talked to me. Telsa went up to him, nudging him and wagging her tail.

Amazingly and instantly, he completely changed and asked me inside, made a coffee. Although we didn't know it at the time, that was the start of things getting much better; Joe, his dad and I from then on started being much more civilized to each other.

Telsa licked Joe's father and sat on his feet, which absolutely melted him. He said he could feel tingling coming up his feet and legs from Telsa and didn't understand what it was about. This didn't seem like the right time to start talking about healing – we had only just managed to get inside the house. I would save the explanation until a more appropriate time. In the meantime, Telsa was working her magic. She had done it again. She was also, of course, delighted to be with Joe. I left two hours later knowing that from now on I would be able to come to the house and have a coffee and take Joe out without all the hassle we'd been going through previously. What a relief that was for me and how wonderful for all four of us.

Thank you, Archangel Michael.

~

The next time I went up to Tynemouth, two weeks later, I was surprised when Joe's father asked if he could come out with Joe and me!

We went out for a lovely meal and everything went much easier than I would ever have imagined possible.

Joe's father had previously been like a wounded animal, aggressive and frightened. He had been struggling with walking and exercise for the past year and was about to have a back operation. I agreed to stay at the house for a few weeks to take care of him after the operation. This was the opportunity for him to experience and start to understand about healing. He had always been a sceptic and made fun of anything I said or did on the subject, but now Telsa was helping him to see and feel that there was healing energy before his very eyes.

Telsa was healing Joe, his dad and me all at the same time, aided by the angels. It was so good to get this family relationship back on track. We all seemed to get on so much better now as friends rather than when we were trying to live together. I was happy because I had my son back part-time and a really good friendship with his father. It had taken three years but miracles had eventually happened. A disastrous relationship had transformed into a good friendship.

At the Nursing Home

I had recently been introduced to a massage therapist, Angela, from Congleton and she had asked me for some healing. We began to exchange therapies and became very good friends. She would do Indian head massage for me and I would do the angelic reiki healing for her.

I was asked to do some healing work in a local nursing home in Macclesfield, Cheshire by Angela, who arranged activities for the residents there. This was the first time I had worked in a nursing home and I was very excited about doing healing for the patients and staff.

I asked if it would be all right to take Telsa with me and explained to the staff that she attended all my teaching groups. The nurse in charge said we should see how it went. So off we were again, Telsa and I, on another adventure.

The first time we went to the nursing home, Telsa chose whom we went to see and talk to. She instinctively knew the people who needed healing, even though they weren't necessarily the ones who appeared to want healing. The residents loved her and, seeing their faces, it didn't take me long to realize that they didn't need me there except to accompany Telsa; it was Telsa who was doing the job and I was merely the assistant! It was wonderful to see Telsa coming into her own with her healing, and I was now allowing her free rein.

This particular day was Staff Healing Day. Quite a few of the nurses and care workers had been watching Telsa and me work with the residents during our previous visits, and were very in-

TELSA

terested to get to know us. The first nurse who came along said she would like some healing but couldn't come in because she was afraid of dogs. Telsa did look a bit intimidating, especially if you were afraid of dogs; she was not like your typical healer dog – small, quiet, timid and shy. Telsa was large, confident, alert and made her presence felt.

I asked Angela to keep Telsa with her while I was healing the nurse and Telsa reluctantly followed Angela.

My patient nervously came into the room and I told her Telsa was with Angela. I sat her down and explained about the healing energy: that it was available to all of us and I would be channelling it from the universe and the angels and bringing it down through my arms and hands, to both her aura and her physical body. I put on a CD of relaxing angelic music and began the healing. All was going really well until I saw Telsa quietly creeping into the room. She had somehow managed to open the door. When Telsa decided to come over and gently sit on my patient's feet, there was nothing I could do; I couldn't stop my healing and had to just keep going. I had no idea what might happen, but my patient didn't seem to notice. All was going well so far. As the healing was coming to a close, I began to wonder what on earth my nervous patient's re-action would be to Telsa not only being in the healing room but actually sitting on her feet. I just trusted and put it out of my mind.

Just as we were finishing the healing Telsa got up, gently put her head on my patient's knee and looked up at her with those big brown, gentle, loving eyes that could melt any heart. To my amaze-ment the nurse just stroked Telsa as though she had always loved dogs. She was so thankful that her fear of dogs had suddenly dis-appeared. I was relieved too! Once again my journey with Telsa had been proven to be anything but boring. The only person who didn't seem to know what was going on in that situation was me!

On another session with the old people in the nursing home, just before Christmas, Angela had organized an accordion player and asked if I would sing Christmas songs and carols with him for the residents and staff. Off we went, with Telsa in tow, to sing for these (hopefully) receptive patients. We started downstairs, where the residents were only physically infirm and were keen to join in the festivities. They joined in with the songs performed by me and Harry the accordionist. They also enjoyed the fuss and love they could give to and get from Telsa.

All was going well, then, until we went upstairs to the patients who were mentally ill. Some of these patients were severely physically and mentally disabled and didn't seem to notice if anyone was there or not, bless them. We just carried on singing anyway, hoping they would enjoy it at some level. The three of us arrived at one particular room occupied by two gentlemen. One was asleep and the other was very distressed and frustrated; he kept ringing the bell for the doctor and shouting. He didn't want anyone else – we tried to ask if he would like a carol or a song, but in no uncertain terms he indicated that he only wanted the doctor. No music or singing would pacify him, but we kept trying anyway. We were just about to give up when Telsa went over to him, put her head on his knee and looked up at him. I was worried in case he became angry with her, but there was no need. It was amazing. We could just see his heart melt and a big smile came over his face. He had forgotten all his pain and distress and just smiled and stroked Telsa. He had forgotten all about the doctor, stopped shouting and sat with Telsa for a good while. Then he went peacefully to sleep.

After Christmas we went to the home again to do some more healing. By now some of the patients who hadn't tried the healing or been interested before were becoming curious and coming over to ask for healing and to see Telsa.

There was one particular man, probably only in his early forties, who used a wheelchair. He had never said a word to us or to any of the staff on any of our visits. In fact, I found out, although he had been there for three years he had had no visitors and had never spoken a word to anyone, staff or patients.

I had noticed though that he had been watching us.

I asked him if he would like some healing, but he didn't answer me. Telsa, though, not put off, went over to him, put her head on his knee and looked up at him, wagging her tail.

Again, she melted someone's heart. The man began to stroke her and started to talk about his childhood. He'd had a black and white collie dog. Here he was, beginning to tell his life story to all of us. This was the first time anyone in the home had had any communication with him and the staff were truly amazed.

By now, as you can imagine, Telsa was gaining a reputation for being there when people needed her and for knowing what to do.

We went to the home one day a week and Telsa couldn't wait to get in there, running in, going up to all the patients in turn and greeting them before I had even got inside. They really loved her, and to see their faces was a wonderful sight. I thought again more than once that they didn't really need me there – Telsa was doing an admirable job by herself. She had found her vocation. I was so proud to be her owner and keeper.

Our Sudden Return
to Newcastle

Telsa and I were just getting into our stride at the nursing home when, sadly, it was all cut short. I was singing in a choir at this time and had just been in Germany with them. I had been speaking to Joe's father the night before, as he had phoned to wish me a great concert. He would not have considered doing anything like this in the past and it was a welcome sign of our rekindled friendship.

On the early-morning flight from Berlin back to Manchester I had noticed a strong energy come to me, but because it was about 5 a.m. and I was so tired – too tired to recognize the energy for what it was – I asked the spirit world to stand back and I would deal with it later. I was so tired due to a very disturbed night at the hotel in Berlin where we had been staying. The hotel had been a hospital during the war and there were hundreds of stuck spirits there, so I had been awake for most of the night, being used again by the spirit world to help these souls to pass over to the light.

As I arrived into Manchester airport my phone rang. It was my son Joe. I couldn't understand what he was saying. I asked him to take some deep breaths and try again and he told me he thought his father was dead. Joe had been shouting up the stairs to him to get him up, and when he didn't answer Joe had gone into the bedroom and found him. Joe was traumatized and in shock. I knew I had to get to Newcastle as quickly as possible. I asked Joe to contact his uncle to come to the house and promised that I would be there in a couple of hours. I then realized that on some level Joe's father must have known that he was about to pass over, and that was why I had received such an unusually lovely phone call from him the previous night.

I went straight away to pick Telsa up from my friend Lynn's house. Off we went, Telsa and I, to do one of our most important jobs to date. I just knew Telsa would do more for Joe than I could ever do. Yes, I could talk to him and be company for him, but Telsa would get much much closer to him and I knew it.

I asked the angels to help me to fly safely in my car to Newcastle. Outside lane all the way and I did it in record time. Joe was in shock when I arrived. He immediately went to his room, taking Telsa with him, which was the right thing under the circumstances.

Telsa did a marvellous job with Joe in the immediate aftermath of his father's death. Just on a practical level, taking her to the beach for walks was great therapy for him. Joe knew that she was healing him in other ways too. She never left his side.

A few weeks after the funeral, things were settling down and I began to wonder why I had been brought back to Newcastle so quickly. Maybe the angels knew I wouldn't go back to live there by choice, so they gave me no choice and at some level I realized there was work to do here.

Telsa and I travelled up and down the motorway between Cheshire and Newcastle for over a year as I had twelve-month courses arranged in Cheshire and Yorkshire and couldn't leave the area. I was on the road most of the time and was finding it exhausting; I was glad when finally I could settle in one place, even though Newcastle wasn't really where I wanted to be. I knew that Telsa and I were there for Joe and to get him on track with a life of his own and that would take time.

Joe and I moved from the big house in Tynemouth and bought a small house each, so that we could be close together but also have our independence.

It worked very well as Joe could be there for Telsa while I was abroad, and wanted to share more fully in her life again.

Things were working wonderfully well now; Joe and I were spending more time together than we had before, but also allowing each other our freedom.

I began to arrange workshops at home in Newcastle and the surrounding areas, in Carlisle and North Yorkshire and, occasionally, in Cheshire.

Telsa became more involved with my groups and without me realizing, was receiving all the activations and attunements to the masters and angels of light just like everyone else on the courses and workshops.

I was very glad to have Telsa on board with me at this stage; I was beginning to work on karmic clearing and clearing dark energies from my patients, and was finding her energy essential as the work became more involved and more intensive.

The First Christmas after Joe's Dad's Passing

Joe and I always knew that this was going to be a difficult time, but we forced ourselves to put a tree up and get ready for Christmas. Joe was still very emotionally fragile and Christmas didn't make things easier as 25 December had also been his father's birthday. Christmas time always brings up all the emotions we have about our lost loved ones. Even though I knew what I knew about the spirit world and that we don't die, rather we pass on to another place, keeping the spirit or soul alive and able to contact our loved ones, it was still hard for me to make Joe feel better. He had "seen" his father coming down the stairs after his passing and that had really freaked him out.

Joe did not get out of bed on the morning of Christmas Eve. It got to 11 a.m. and he was still up there, so I went to his room and asked how he was. He said he was fine but I knew he wasn't, even though Telsa was snuggling in to him on his bed. I took him a cup of tea and said that his dad would be with him for Christmas. He couldn't deal with that so I didn't say any more. I was aware that his father was telling me at that moment to tell Joe he really was with him this Christmas and that he loved him very much. I, in my head, told Joe's father to leave it as it wasn't a good time. His father's timing had never been the best, especially in an emotional situation like this one.

Joe and I continued just talking about the past, funny things, anything we could think of. I said we could watch *Jack Frost*, the

54

film he had loved when he was younger. It's about a boy whose musician father dies but comes back as a snowman who comes to life so that he can be with his son again for a while.

Just then I felt a big surge of energy and a build-up of it around Telsa. Unbelievably, the image of a snowman appeared on the wall. Telsa, who was still lying on the bed with Joe, sat up and moved her head from side to side, which Joe obviously saw. Telsa could see the snowman too. It was Joe's father, determined that I tell Joe his message. I couldn't manage to hold it back, it was so strong. I told Joe what had happened and he began to cry, saying "Don't tell me any more." I began to cry and went downstairs realizing that I had upset Joe even more. I was cross with Joe's dad for doing that at a very sensitive time. Within two minutes, though, Joe had followed me downstairs, and he put his arms round me and said he was sorry. As he had watched Telsa's reaction he'd realized that what I'd told him must have been true. I think that incident, even though it was upsetting, in a funny kind of way made him feel better.

Again, although I'd thought it wasn't the right time to tell Joe about his dad, the spirit world knows better than we do, and we have to remember that.

The inevitable was almost upon us – it was Christmas Day tomorrow and we were going to have to face it together. Lewis's mum Judy had invited us both round to their house for Christmas lunch, which seemed that it would save the day.

I wasn't sure whether Joe would actually manage to go to Judy's on Christmas morning until I told him Telsa was ready; he then got himself together and off we went, the three of us. Lewis was Joe's closest friend and he was trying his best to keep his spirits up. Joe couldn't have been with anyone better that day; Telsa and Lewis, his closest friends, meant the world to him. The irony here was that, not many years later, Joe was to lose both of these precious friends within months of each other.

~

We had decided to sprinkle some of Joe's father's ashes out at sea, and a friend organized for us to go out on a lifeboat to do this. The day we had arranged was a very cold, icy and windy one in February. The lifeboat skipper rang to say that the sea was very rough and did we want to postpone it, as they thought it would be too traumatic for me.

I decided we had to go ahead, though, as I was afraid that if it were put off Joe would not be persuaded again to do it. Off we went: Joe, his uncle and me. We had to put on padded life-suits, helmets and boots – we walked and looked like spacemen. This really made us laugh and eased the situation somewhat. We got into the lifeboat and set off to sea amidst the rolling waves. It was very rough indeed – it was so bad that I asked Archangel Michael to pick us up and save us if we were thrown out of the boat. We went out quite far, as the lifeboat crew explained that we had to get a good way out from the shore to scatter the ashes.

Joe and his uncle looked ill, probably partly because of the motion of the boat but also because of the sad occasion. I felt so sorry for them, thinking about how hard it must be for both of them losing a father and a brother.

We eventually stopped, the water up to our knees in the boat. I passed the ashes in their casket to Joe and we and the crew all held on to his legs while he leaned overboard to scatter them. The wind blew them all over the place and Joe nearly ended up overboard. I had some angel sprinkles, small gold foil "confetti" in the shape of angels, which I scattered. I had bought some white roses for us to place on the water too, but it was so rough that I ended up just throwing them all overboard. Then we had to make the journey back. Joe and his uncle were looking dreadful by this time, and I was so busy seeing to them that I forgot about the dangerousness of the trip.

Eventually we got off the boat and the two of them said that they'd been so busy trying to stay in the boat and were so scared that they couldn't think about their father and brother, worrying instead about whether they would ever get back to the shore safe and sound! It was particularly funny because Joe's uncle had been an engineer in the navy, and Joe was usually such a strong character.

As we were getting our life-suits off we all burst out laughing at the situation, and that was the start of turning the corner for all of us. We laugh now whenever we talk about it. Joe's dad had the last laugh, I think, that day, and Archangel Michael really did protect us. One day Joe and I were busy talking about his father when I suddenly realized that we had left the rest of the ashes in the garage of the old house in Tynemouth. I immediately telephoned the new owners of the house, to be told that they had emptied everything into a skip. So off I went to rescue him. There he was in the skip, still in the jar, and all intact.

Joe and I laughed and laughed, and it was exactly what we'd needed. We decided to put the rest of the ashes under a bush or a tree in the garden. I said to Joe that it was his dad's way of being part of all this and letting us know that he was still around. All of this really lifted a very sombre situation. Amazing in what ways the spirit world works to get us through these very challenging times.

Opening Hearts

The caravan was beautiful in the wintertime, with the snow covering the hills and treetops and lining both sides of the river. It was like a wonderful winter wonderland from a Christmas card. My friend Nadine was staying overnight with us and we had a lovely meal and settled down for a cosy night surrounded by candles and my angels. We were talking about spiritual things, as we usually did.

Telsa was sitting on the settee right next to Nadine when I began to feel a surge of energy and see that familiar bright white light building up around the dog. I just knew something was about to happen. Nadine had been feeling that she was stuck on her pathway and still dealing with a past hurtful relationship. The energy now began to build up over and behind my friend and I realized that the healing had started without me. There were two masters with my friend, one holding her while the other held her heart, healing it. I asked if she could feel anything and I think she was just about to say no, when there was another surge of energy and she said yes, she could really feel it and needed to lie down. Telsa was again engineering another major healing session that we weren't prepared for. The masters were Jesus and Mary Magdalene. The healing went on for about half an hour and Telsa lay completely still throughout. Nadine went on her way the following morning refreshed and ready to move forward. She knew the person who had instigated this healing and gave her a massive hug. Telsa was delighted. That was the only reward she needed.

I had been doing an angelic healing course in Stoke-on-Trent. While I was there, a client who I will call Lynsey, who had previously been on one of my groups, came along for a one-to-one session shortly after giving birth to her new baby. She had had healing sessions while she was pregnant and it had helped her and the baby very much. Telsa as usual wanted to see the baby, and made a gentle fuss. We started the healing for Lynsey and her gorgeous, new little boy. When we had finished the healing I asked her if she had a problem with her big toe. She said she had and that Telsa had been sitting on it all through the session. She could feel intense heat and a tingling moving around the toe and all the way up her leg. She knew Telsa was doing her job. As I'd had my eyes closed I hadn't noticed Telsa sitting on Lynsey's feet, but we had obviously both been picking up on the same complaint.

Joe's father in the early days was, bless him, one of the world's biggest sceptics. One of my hardest challenges in more ways than one. He couldn't understand at first why I was wasting my time on all this "mumbo jumbo" as he called it. It was Telsa who managed to get through to him. When she sat on his feet he would feel the heat and tingling and he didn't know what to think. He couldn't explain it but he was beginning to believe that something was happening and the energy was coming from a higher force. He reached a point where he was happy to have us both do healing on him, after coming home from hospital after a major back operation. Telsa would lie with him while I also gave him healing. He would feel the tingling sensation and it helped him cope with the pain and discomfort. Telsa and I based ourselves at his house when he came out of hospital, as he was in need of care and attention. Amazingly for him, he allowed Telsa to sleep on his bed. This was a first, but he said he could feel the tingling and heat moving up and down his back. He knew she was healing him even though he still couldn't really explain it. He began to get much better and was back to doing most of his normal jobs very soon. Telsa had done it again – managed to open a heart and make a believer out of a real sceptic. I firmly believe that this enabled Joe's father to pass over more easily when it was his time.

Telsa opened another heart on one of our regular walks. We regularly met other dedicated dog walkers in the fields near our house and both we and our animals would socialize.

Jim, and Bruno his dog, were two of the regulars in our walking group. Bruno was seventeen years old, a "Heinz 57" variety. Whilst he was really quite fit for his age, he wasn't keen on other dogs around him. He was OK with Telsa though, as she would greet him and then give him his own space. Jim had recently lost his wife and was devastated. He was inconsolable and Telsa and I had to allow him to go through this stage of grief and just listen. We would sit on a seat and talk while Telsa would sit on his feet. Jim didn't know what was happening but Telsa did. I was doing the counselling and Telsa the healing, and I feel sure that Jim didn't have a clue or he would have reacted with scepticism and not have walked or sat with us.

He asked me about my job and what it entailed. I told him about the healing and the angels. He looked at me, speechless, and I said that was how most people reacted when I told them about my work. He smiled and said he was fine with it as long as I didn't try to make him believe it.

One day soon after this, Jim told me that he had seen a bright white light in his room and felt that it was his late wife. This was a breakthrough. And it happened more than once. A few days later he had a fall and was housebound. Telsa and I went round to his house and I asked if he would like some healing for his legs. He was a bit reluctant but eventually we persuaded him to have some healing.

Not too long after this, Jim passed away himself and it was wonderful knowing that he had connected to his wife and the angels before his journey to the other side.

We can do so much for older people by telling them about angels and the spirit world. They may not appear to be listening but you can be sure the spirit world and the angels would not miss a chance to connect to them and to enable them to have an easier passing when the time comes.

Not long after Joe's father had passed over, Joe and his best friend Lewis were in the house one evening. Lewis was close to Telsa too; she would sit at his feet, by his side or on his knee and I always knew she was doing her job without being noticed. Somehow we started talking about healing and angels and what I was doing. Joe was already familiar with all of this and I'm sure he had mentioned it to Lewis.

Lewis was interested but a bit nervous about it all. He started to tell me about the spirit people he was seeing in the house while he was living with his father. He didn't know what it was all about and was a bit fearful. I tried to explain that as it was an old house the spirits were probably one or more of the previous residents, stuck between the two worlds, especially if they had died suddenly. Lewis was feeling somewhat insecure, not knowing who these spirits were, so I told him about Archangel Michael, the angel of strength, courage and protection, and gave him a picture of him to put under his pillow or under his bed to make him feel safe. He wasn't ready to go any further with this but was happy to let Archangel Michael – and Telsa! – help him.

Terribly, a few years later, in 2009, Lewis was to pass away suddenly at the tender age of twenty-seven. Such a shock and a devastating time for his mum Judy, his brother Paul and the rest of his family, and also for his best friend Joe.

Joe had really had to push himself to go with Paul to check on Lewis's flat the following week. There he found the picture of Archangel Michael under Lewis's bed, the very picture I had given him a few years before. Joe was so excited to tell me, amidst his grief, as he knew Lewis would be well looked after now that he had connected with the angels.

It was devastating for Joe, after he had just about recovered from the passing of his father and Telsa. Joe and Lewis had been inseparable, like brothers or even more so, since they had met at four years old. They saw each other nearly every day and always spoke on the phone more than once a day too. This was to be much more difficult for Joe than his father's passing, as the connection was so strong between him and Lewis. I felt thankful and blessed that Lewis had taken the previous talks about spirits and the angels on board.

When Lewis passed I was constantly sending him light and the violet flame, which is a special dispensation to us from our creator. I know this helped him to connect with St Germain, Ascended Master and alchemist who has lived previous lives as Christopher Columbus, Joseph the father of Jesus, Merlin and le Comte de St Germain, the eighteenth-century "Wonderman of Europe", to name but a few. St Germain is keeper of the violet flame, which transmutes negative energies into positive light and so clears negativity from our physical and energetic bodies.

Lewis has sent me messages to say that he was being healed in the violet flame and is now beginning to work, from the other side, as a guide to Joe and to his family.

In the earlier days, Telsa and I would stay at the caravan in Knaresborough when we were doing workshops in York. Not everyone at that time was happy to accommodate dogs, especially a large boxer. I also used it as a halfway house when I was visiting Joe in Newcastle. I met a gentleman there, whom I will call Bill, who was living at the caravan park alone. He had been admitted to a psychiatric hospital a few years back but was now able to live in the community. He was struggling to get his mind together and would get muddled and very depressed. We, Telsa and I, met him while we were walking in the fields and he asked if he could come with us, and began gradually to get close to Telsa. We sometimes shared a coffee at my caravan or his. I knew he was a very gentle man underneath all the trauma and Telsa would definitely make sure that I was not under any threat. I would have known from her reactions if not.

He began asking me what I did for a job, and when I told him I did healing work with angels he went very quiet. I told him not to worry – I was used to getting that response. He started to tell me all the things that had been happening to him. His visions and "happenings". How he was having visions and he couldn't tell anyone in case they admitted him to the psychiatric hospital again.

We became good friends and he began to call to me from his caravan when he had had another experience. He was on a very difficult pathway, that was for sure. On this particular evening Telsa and I were in the field where his caravan was sited and he spotted us and came outside. He told me that he had been given instruction from St Cuthbert in a vision to go to Holy Island. There was something he had to do there; he did not know what it was but had been told he had to go soon. He was beginning to prepare for this trip and was on a mission to get there; it seemed to energize him as he began over the following days to do more walking. The more he accepted his spirituality, the freer he was becoming from the terrible pain he had been suffering before. I could see a big change in his physical appearance and his face was beginning to glow. He asked if he could sometimes take Telsa while I was busy, and she was happy to go with him for a walk and to sit with him in his caravan.

One evening Telsa and I met him in the field and he said he could see a bright violet light all around me, going up to the sky. He said it was a saint with me but didn't know any more than that. I knew it was St Germain as I had been sending Bill the violet-flame energy to transmute the lower energies around him.

The last I saw of him, he was a much more handsome and upright man, on his way to Holy Island. I had to sell my caravan suddenly when I moved to Newcastle after Joe's father's death, so wasn't able to catch up with him. I haven't seen him since and often wonder how he got on. I feel sure that he is doing what he is meant to be doing now and believing in himself.

More of Telsa's Healing

I was running one of my first courses in angelic healing at my house in Newcastle. There were five of us, or six counting Telsa, who was becoming a more and more important member of my groups.

This particular weekend I had known that a group member, Laura, was having a very difficult time with her family and her job. She and her boss were in conflict and she was to be suspended.

She also had a family of three children who were all dependent on her income, and she was trying to make a go of things on her own. She was a qualified counsellor and was training in complementary therapies and angels. Laura came to me to train on the British healers course and in angelic healing. During this time she was in need of healing herself; I could see that and Telsa knew it too.

We had started the angelic reiki course and Telsa, this day in the early days of her healings, had decided to stay out in the hallway. We had all gone through the meditations, clearings and attunements and were starting to do partner healings with all the members of the group. As we had five members in the group, I suggested we use Telsa to make up the numbers, and asked Laura if she would partner with Telsa. Just then Telsa, without being fetched or called, just walked in and plonked herself down on Laura's feet. Laura was amazed and burst into tears; Telsa had started to do her work already and even knew who she was working with.

That was the beginning of a fresh journey for Laura's healing, and now she has found her vocation and is successfully running her own counselling and healing groups.

On another occasion, Peter was attending one of my sound healing groups. He had been under enormous pressure from his parents and at college. He was mildly autistic and, although he was doing his best, I could see that he was struggling to focus. He had a lot going on in his life for such a young soul. Telsa came to sit on his feet, which seemed to make him calmer. He had complained of a back problem and was suffering badly today. I thought it was possibly caused or made worse by all the stress he was under.

It was coming up to lunchtime and I was just thinking that I would need to get him out of the group and home if there was no improvement, when Telsa turned around and stretched up to him, placing her front legs round his neck. Peter's face changed. Telsa was healing him; he started feeling much better and was able to stay for the afternoon session. I don't know exactly what Telsa did, but her magic seemed to be working and that was fine by me.

I had been invited to attend and participate in an event in Bournemouth with Diana Cooper. I badly wanted to go but was finding it difficult, as Joe and his partner were going to be out of the country on holiday, leaving me with no one to look after Telsa. Diana kindly said that she would be happy to have Telsa stay over, so off we started on the train from Newcastle to Bournemouth with a suitcase, my crystal bowls and Telsa. I tried not to think how we would manage this journey and knew Telsa would do as much as she could to smooth the adventure.

The train was crowded but we were fortunate, with some help from the angels; we had been booked into a disabled seat with plenty of legroom. At the next stop we were joined by a lady who had lost her boxer dog just a few months earlier. She loved Telsa and talked about her own dog. She laughed and she cried, while Telsa lay on her feet all the while. She felt so much better by the time we arrived in London.

The return journey was not going to be as easy. The train was packed to overflowing. There was no room for Telsa to get comfortable, so I gave our seat up and tried to stand by the door, which was much easier. There was a young woman right next to where we were standing and when she saw Telsa she screamed. Her boyfriend said she was terrified of dogs and I told him she wouldn't hurt his girlfriend. Without me noticing, Telsa decided to get under the seat and sit on the woman's feet. She didn't even realize for a while that Telsa was there – I had realized but thought it would cause more fuss if I did anything about it. Telsa was doing her thing and I just had to leave her to it. Telsa then put her head on the woman's knee, giving her a bit of a shock when she first saw those big brown eyes staring up at her, but Telsa had already done enough to relax her and make her feel at ease. I then spotted two seats in the next carriage. They were reserved and the seats' owners were due to get on at the next stop, but I decided to take my chance and ask the angels that if it was for everyone's highest good, would those people not get on this train. My prayers were answered and Telsa and I were able to take the seats for the rest of the journey home to Newcastle. I feel that was our reward from the angels for the healing work Telsa and I had done.

Telsa Helping
with M.E.

While I was doing an angel course in Manchester, a lovely lady who I will call Susan asked me if she could do the course with me. She was very drawn to it but as she had M.E., she didn't know whether she would be strong enough to complete it.

I talked to her for a while and knew from the angels that I had to get Susan to try to do the course and that I would have to take the responsibility as things unfolded.

We started the course that evening and I knew that, as it was a short session, it would be all right. I thought that if I could attune her to the first degree of the course it would be a step in the right direction.

We started the course and I could see that Susan was very weak and struggling to be there with us, but because she was making so much effort to do it it felt like the right thing to do; as though it was meant to be. Telsa knew there was something she needed to do too and immediately came up to lie with Susan. Susan seemed to enjoy Telsa's company and I think it took her mind off not feeling well. The evening session went well but I was wondering if we would see her again for the whole-day session the next day. I knew that, if she arrived, with the angels and Telsa's help she would get through it.

The next morning Susan did arrive, but was very weak, saying that she didn't know whether she should have come.

This was my first challenge of this kind and I had to just ask for guidance from the angels. I advised her to relax, take in what was happening and not worry about trying too hard, and assured her that she could leave at any time. Telsa was again lying on her feet.

Everyone else arrived and we made a start for the day. As we moved on, Telsa still lying with Susan, she seemed to be improving. I noticed a shift in her energy; it was becoming lighter, and I felt that we were getting somewhere. As the day progressed I could feel that she was moving in the right direction. We did the healing sessions and Telsa was still by her side.

The following morning, the last day of the course, Susan came in looking like a different person. She had healed whatever was holding her back and was working just the same as the others. I was delighted and so was Telsa. Telsa stayed close by Susan but was not lying on her feet any more. I think she was allowing Susan to move forward herself now, and standing back a little.

By the end of the course Susan was thrilled that she had managed to complete it, and touched and moved by how compassionate and caring the other members of the group and Telsa had been to her.

It was the end of a perfect day for Telsa and me.

PART III

Other Animals and Nature

In Nature

While I was living in Alsager in Cheshire, Telsa and I had found some lovely walks, which we did twice a day. There was a walk through the fields and by the river that we particularly enjoyed.

One day I noticed a loud whirring noise, a sort of loud whisper, as we were walking by the river. Telsa noticed it too. We both looked around, but could not see anything different. The water was still and there was no wind. I couldn't move on until I had found out what it was. I turned to look at the trees by the river and just knew that one particular tree was "calling" to me. I thought I was going a bit crazy as I hadn't heard trees speaking before! There was no wind but this tree was moving. As I looked closer I noticed that it had beautiful heart-shaped roots at the base of the trunk, coming out of the earth. Telsa was pulling over to it too, which made me think that she was also feeling something.

To my amazement, this tree was telling me that it had come to support me for the teacher-training course I was attending in France the following month. It was sending me lots of love, support and courage for my trip.

Telsa and I then started to visit this tree every day. It was so loving, and it gave me the strength day by day to feel comfortable and more confident. It was a wonderful happening that I will never forget. Telsa could obviously feel the loving nature spirits around this tree, as she would sit there happily for as long as I liked.

Just before I went to France I again took Telsa to our tree. We stayed for a while, resting in its loving energy. I was beginning to feel the nature spirits very strongly. I said to the tree that I would be straight back to see it with Telsa when I arrived home from France.

As part of the course we all had to write a story, and mine was about my special tree, with its heart-shaped roots and nature spirits. When I arrived home three weeks later, I couldn't wait to get Telsa back from my niece and take her along to see our tree, to tell it about the story and all that had happened in France

We couldn't find it! We looked everywhere. Then I realized to my horror that I could see tree stumps; someone had been chopping down the trees while I was away. I also hadn't realized that it was on the railway embankment. They had destroyed our special tree and our dream. What a shock! I was so upset that I began to cry. It may seem strange that I was so upset over a tree, but it had been a very special connection, for both me and Telsa, to the nature kingdom. One we would never forget.

Telsa Plays with Elementals

For a while Joe and I lived very close to the Jesmond Dene park, which was a beautiful place to walk dogs. Joe and I walked there most days with Telsa. One day, she began to play about in the bushes, and moved her head backwards and forwards and bounded back and forth as she did when she had seen something unusual. I realized she was playing with elementals; fairies, gnomes and other similar beings. Even though I couldn't always see them myself, I could feel them at the moment, making my body tingle. I could also see the grass moving on its own. Whenever I could see or feel the presence of elementals, I would check to see if Telsa had noticed and she always had. She would look intently at them and move her head from side to side. I think she was trying to play with them.

Joe even remarked one day that the grass was moving on its own, and asked me what it was. I told him it was the elementals, fairies playing in the bushes and by the water. He couldn't actually see them but could feel the tingling too.

Telsa and Cats

Telsa loved to chase cats; not to hurt them but for the game and the fun of it all. When, occasionally, a cat she had been chasing stopped and let her catch up, it would be pleasantly surprised when it turned out that Telsa just wanted to sniff around it. Telsa used to stay with my niece Ursula in Cheshire sometimes while I was working away, and Ursula had two kittens, who loved to play and jump about. Telsa would go to sleep with the kittens tucked up in to her body. They really loved each other.

One day I was at the house of a client called John. I had gone to give him some healing with Telsa as he had recently lost his wife and was struggling to move forward. He had a cat called Charlie who was a bit of a character.

The first time we'd gone to John's house, Charlie had come charging over from where he'd been sitting and Telsa went running towards him to chase him. Charlie was not, it seemed, like most cats Telsa met; he stood still, and when Telsa moved nearer to him, Charlie darted forward and chased Telsa around the garden. Telsa didn't know what was happening, but she must have realized very quickly that this was no ordinary cat, and they were always wary of each other after that.

This particular day, Telsa and I went into the house to do the healing. Telsa sat on John's feet and off we went with some beautiful music for the healing session. We were about ten minutes into the session when Charlie appeared through the catflap and Telsa got up and chased him back outside. While all this was happening, John was thankfully oblivious to it and continued to enjoy the music and the healing. I just carried on, hoping things would settle down and I could finish the healing without too much disturbance.

A short time later Telsa came back into the room and again sat on John's feet. We were coming to the close of the healing now, but then Charlie appeared in the room again. Fortunately, I was able to bring John quickly back to the present before the chasing and the disturbance could start all over again. However, this time when Charlie darted forward at Telsa, for once she didn't react; she stayed on John's feet. Perhaps she had realized that this was Charlie's house and he was going to make her respect that fact; and perhaps Telsa was letting him know in return that she was busy doing a healing session. Two strong characters, they had each met their match!

John had had a very comfortable, relaxing healing, although Telsa, Charlie and I were just about worn out and maybe in need of some healing ourselves. Healing has never been a dull occupation with Telsa around!

~

After Telsa had passed on 7 May 2009, a friend contacted me, desperate for some healing. Her cat had managed to get out of the house and had been hit by a car. She had bolted and hidden, possibly badly wounded, under the next-door neighbour's garden shed, and whatever my friend tried she wouldn't come out from under it. I started doing the healing immediately and, straight away, Telsa's spirit came to me BIG TIME. I should have known she wouldn't pass up a chance to do something with a cat. I "sent" Telsa's spirit to help entice the cat out from under the shed and we completed the healing.

A little later my friend called to say that her cat was fine, and had just been treated by the vet for shock and bruising. She said that her cat had shot out from under the shed and into the house like a bolt of lightning, and if she hadn't known better she would have sworn it was Telsa who had chased her. We both laughed when I told her about the healing and Telsa's spirit.

One of my neighbours had a large ginger cat, who used to love tormenting Telsa by sitting on the fence between our house and next-door. This cat never dared come down to the ground in our garden while Telsa was alive, but as soon as Telsa had passed over he somehow knew she was gone, and was in the garden like a flash.

Our animals are so naturally tuned into spirit.

PIPPA

The very first thing I noticed about Telsa was her quiet calm energy, especially remarkable for a boxer. She seemed to have this ability to be able to "read" people, like she knew what they were thinking.

If she felt they needed love she would go up to them and give them a friendly lick, or just encourage them to stroke her. If she thought they needed space then she would give that until they inevitably came round to her patient, gentle energy. What I always witnessed, however, was people smiling when they were around her. She united people.

I feel that she acted as a grounding energy for Rosemary in her workshops. To me Telsa was much more than just a dog – whenever I looked into her eyes the unconditional love looking back at me told me that.

I am sure Telsa is still around Rosemary, still doing her healing work, because her energy on Earth was too strong to just have a "holiday" in the spirit world.

DECLAN

It is strange sometimes how we can close ourselves down and not really realize we have done it. I suppose it is because we're preoccupied, thinking of other things, or maybe we are feeling especially vulnerable or out of sorts and we're not liking ourselves or other people a lot.

Telsa was sensitive to these kinds of moods and was especially good at knowing when people around her were out of sorts. I have known her respond to me in these moods and I have noticed her respond to others when they were in a similar way.

What she would do is suss you out, and then gently, but quite directly, move in front of you and put her head on your knee. In any kind of mood it is hard to resist the appeal that a loving dog can put into the way she or he is looking at you. With Telsa it was the look along with the unconditional way she acted. It didn't matter how you were feeling about yourself, she was going to give you love and attention! It would be hard not to stroke her and to be reminded of how good that feels – because in the act of lifting my arms and moving towards her I would be opening up to receiving her love and opening up to letting that love flow.

Of course, thinking back over this now, it is a lot more obvious to me that once we allow ourselves to receive and give love we are in the flow of life; with that flow we can begin to feel good about ourselves, and from there begin to feel good about others and about life in general.

Telsa understood all this, instinctively, and was always there unconditionally to help us feel good about ourselves.

What a healer!

I remember distinctly the first time it crossed my mind that Telsa might be a healer. There was a group of us practising spiritual healing in Harrogate. Telsa was in the room and was stretched out, enjoying the energies. After a little while I became aware that she had shifted her position and was lying at a tangent to someone who was receiving healing from me.

Although Telsa was still lying down, I didn't feel that she was relaxed in the same way as she had been before. Intuitively, I became aware that if Telsa had been a human healer about to start a healing on this person, the position she was in was just exactly right. The energy that she was helping bring in and move around felt just right to me too. Later I noticed she had moved again, this time to underneath the chair of someone else who was receiving healing. This position and energy felt exactly right too.

One of the people above, who Telsa had gone to lie near, said that the spot that Telsa had occupied during their healing had been the source of comforting, loving and "glowing energy".

BARBARA

In one workshop I attended, Telsa had a tummy bug and was much quieter and not her usual sociable self. I felt that she was picking up negative energy from a member of the group, taking it on board herself (where it manifested as the tummy bug) to help this group member transmute the negative energy. She often used to do this. I worked on Telsa to give her healing; she lay for fifteen minutes only occasionally lifting her head to look at me. She knew when it was time to stop; she jumped down from the settee and licked my hand, obviously feeling better.

A beautiful dog, and she is spreading herself and her loving healing energy around even after her passing!

GLENYS

I feel so blessed to have met Telsa and to have experienced her healing presence during one of Rosemary's two-day angelic healing courses. Rosemary is an amazing spiritual teacher and dear friend and the deep bond between her and Telsa was wonderful to see. Throughout the course I greatly appreciated and valued Telsa's friendliness and unique healing involvement.

I loved the way Telsa came forward at various times to help. For example, she kept a peaceful eye on things, coming forward when I needed grounding during one of the sessions. In that moment, I felt deeply aware of her healing abilities, displayed by her purposeful action. I will always remember the look in Telsa's eyes as she sat in front of me for a few minutes, looking at me with peace and love in her eyes, before coming to give me a beautiful hug. To me, she has a "dolphin nature"; there is something wonderful and extraordinary about her.

I am grateful to have experienced, first hand, the healing work and gentle presence of Telsa, working incarnate in a unique partnership with Rosemary.

I do so hope that those reading these insights into Telsa's life will find these stories uplifting, for they stand as a record of a remarkable life. Thank you so much, Telsa. I continue to value your healing work.

Telsa Heals Fear of Dogs

As many people who knew her realized, and as I mentioned earlier, Telsa was not your typical healer dog. She was a large, dark-brindle boxer with white patches on her chest and feet. I'm sure she was more than a little intimidating to many people meeting her for the first time, but she had an amazing way of making people feel at ease with those beautiful big soft brown eyes that could melt any heart.

It is quite unusual for dogs, especially boxers and some other larger breeds, to stare at humans and feel comfortable; staring or direct eye contact is confrontational in their "language" and it can make them nervous. Telsa was strikingly different, right from when she was a puppy; she would eyeball people with those huge brown eyes of hers – I was convinced she was talking telepathically. She would not drop her gaze until she was taken notice of or understood.

She had a small docked tail, which would wag at a hundred miles an hour; I used to imagine the whiplash we would have all suffered if she had had a full tail! Her nature was loving and unconditional; whether you thought you liked dogs or not, she would win you over. She would sit and tune in to people and always seemed to know exactly how to handle that particular person and situation.

There were many times when Telsa came along to one of my healing groups – or should I say *our* healing groups. Sometimes I would forget to mention when organizing the groups that I had a dog, and often one person would say on the day that they were afraid of dogs. I never had to do anything; Telsa would always know straight away and would move so that she was a good distance away from the person, but in front of them, in full view, with her back to them. As the day progressed Telsa would turn sideways to them but still keep her distance. By lunchtime she would be facing them, still lying down, but closer. She would watch for an opportunity – for example if the person became emotional – and would take her cue to slowly move forward, put her head on their knee and look up at them with those big, soft brown eyes. Sometimes, if she felt it was right, she would go right up to them and put her front paws around them to give them a cuddle. It always worked; people who started off scared of dogs ended up being hugged or rested on by Telsa, perfectly happy about it.

PARVEEN

When I first entered Rosemary's living room to do the angelic reiki course, I had no idea that she had a dog. I have had bad experiences with dogs in the past and was therefore frightened to be in the same room as them.

As soon as Rosemary had asked everyone in the room if they were comfortable with dogs I felt a flutter in my chest. I thought of all sorts of excuses to not have the dog in the same room as me. After some persuasion from Rosemary, though, telling us Telsa was a very gentle and friendly dog, I thought she couldn't be that bad. Telsa entered the room and approached each one of us in turn. I had a shock when I saw her as she was so huge. I was expecting something like a poodle, not a big boxer dog. She had a lovely brown coat and her big brown eyes were staring at me. After a while I began to think that she was quite cute, and I even managed to stroke her. At first Telsa kept her distance so that I could get used to her presence, only moving forward slowly and gradually. I knew I had nothing to fear. I felt really comfortable in close proximity to Telsa for the rest of the day, and I realized that she had become my friend.

During the healing practices, we had all done healing on Telsa, and I became quite confident about it. As she lay with the sun shining through the window onto her, her paw rested on my leg to reassure me. I was no longer to be frightened of dogs.

When I broke down with overwhelming emotions– not because I felt ill but because of the unconditional love that I felt in the room – Telsa stayed close to me to comfort me. I felt safe and loved. Rosemary did tell us that Telsa was a healing dog, and I can definitely say I felt healed and reassured.

MARCELLA

I am a healer and I was looking for an angelic reiki master, to learn how to teach angelic reiki myself. I had already done some reiki training, so was more than ready to move forward on my healing/spiritual path.

When I met Rosemary I wanted to book to do her course, but when she told me that her dog Telsa usually joined the groups and was a healer herself, to be honest I was not keen as I was petrified of dogs. I wanted to do the course, though, so booked it anyway.

Rosemary met me off the train and we walked to her car. When she opened the back door to put my case in, there was Telsa. She looked at me with her beautiful, soppy, big brown eyes and I couldn't believe it – I wasn't scared of her. I sat in the front seat of the car with Telsa behind me, and Telsa put her head on my shoulder and kept it there all the way to Rosemary's house.

Telsa had never met me before, but she yet behaved as if she had known me all her life. She made me feel so relaxed before we even got to the group. Telsa seemed to know how to give me the space I needed so I wouldn't be frightened.

As our group session started, she lay down on the floor close to me with her back to me so I wouldn't be scared of her. A little later she put her left paw on my right foot for a while and sent some healing. Then she swapped paws, put her right paw on my left foot and sent healing again. I was absolutely amazed. Telsa spent a lot of time with me throughout the whole weekend and I got really close to her. She is a very special dog and without doubt an angelic reiki master.

I would never have been able to spend time with any other boxer dog like this: I was so scared of them. I know Telsa has been sent from heaven to help heal people and she deserves recognition for what she does.

I asked Rosemary to take a photo of me with Telsa as I knew my family would not believe what had happened over that special weekend. Telsa helped me through all the healings and completely cured my fear of dogs.

After that most beautiful weekend, to mark and re-member the experience of meeting Telsa I bought myself a bronze statue of a little girl kneeling down holding a little puppy. When I am in my garden and I look at it, I think of Telsa.

Vets on the British Healers Courses

When I came back from the teacher-training course with Diana Cooper, in Bergerac, France, I knew things would never be the same for me now and that I was moving rapidly along my spiritual path.

I had met a lovely woman in France, who had told me about a spiritual healing course that would run in Blackpool over the next twelve months, so as soon as I got home I arranged to travel to Blackpool the following month to start the course.

I was very lucky to be able to take Telsa with me, not into the groups but to spend time with everyone at breaks and lunchtimes.

The following year, I began a teacher-training course with the British Healers Association (BHA).

In 2004 I started teaching the BHA course. I had a group in Yorkshire and one in Cheshire. It was all going well.

One day I received a call from Lynn, a member of staff at the Croft Vets Clinic in Stoke-on-Trent. She wanted one of the vets and other members of her practice to train as healers. I was delighted and thought it was a great breakthrough for a veterinary clinic to want to incorporate healing into their practice.

We arranged a date to start and off we went with the course. In the early days I was wary of bringing Telsa into groups in case she was disruptive, but it was different with the vets. They really loved animals and loved having Telsa around, and I'm sure this love is one of the reasons why they were so keen to do the healing course. Telsa did a lot of healing every time we had a session with the vets' group, and it was then that I began to see how naturally she knew who needed healing at any particular time.

The course was very successful and beautiful and I made some very good friends there.

It was not long before Lynn asked if I could run an angelic reiki group for them. This was when Telsa, without me realizing it, really got attuned to the angels and masters. It was almost unbelievable how she just knew when she had to be still and meditate and when she had to heal.

On this course with the vets' group, I had been doing the initial clearing and was ready to do the attunements with all the group members. As I passed Telsa, who had been lying down the whole time, she immediately sat up for me to attune her – she obviously thought that I might otherwise forget she was there. When she was happy that I knew she was there and had attuned her, she lay back down again. I realized then that this was no ordinary dog. She was in the masters group and she was determined to get attuned!

The Vet's Story

. . . .

by Lynn Scott

*This chapter was contributed by Lynn Scott,
manager of the Croft Veterinary Practice,
Stoke-on-Trent. Lynn's vets practice attended a
12-month healing training course with me
for the British Healers Association.*

"Helloooo," said Rosemary, smiling, as she opened the door the first time I met her. "Oh don't mind Telsa, she's a healer too." And as I came to realize over time, she was.

Working with animals in a veterinary clinic is so rewarding, but it is even more so when you can combine healing and other complementary therapies with the conventional work that we do. Animals are very accepting of these therapies as the emphasis is on their needs and choice. However, to meet a dog who was a healer in her own right was really rather special. That was Telsa. A lovely gentle brown-and-white boxer with a way all of her own.

While working towards the British Healers qualification with Rosemary, a small group from the clinic, which included a vet, met regularly to learn, share and perform healing on each other. As a module of the course covers giving healing to animals, it was the perfect opportunity to invite clients and their pets to come along for free healing sessions, carried out by the student healers under Rosemary's supervision.

Telsa came into her own here, choosing to work with those students who were not overly confident with animals and helping them to gain the confidence and quiet understanding required.

On one very special day the fact that Telsa had worked with the group in this way helped a new doggy patient of mine to willingly accept healing from the group and to feel calm and relaxed in what for that dog would normally have been an impossible situation.

I also completed my angelic reiki qualifications with Rosemary and Telsa was present at the attunements. When working with angelic reiki the clearing meditations can be quite powerful, and Telsa would help to ground you after the meditation – but only after asking your permission.

Telsa had many special qualities and as someone who has been able to spend time with her, to receive healing from her and to learn to appreciate my own dog's healing ways, I feel very privileged to have known her.

Telsa and the Crystal Bowls

In 2003 I attended a sound healing day and heard someone play a crystal bowl. I couldn't believe what it did to me and my body: it was as if all my cells were tingling from the top of my head to my toes, which in fact they were! I couldn't wait to find out where to acquire these beautiful instruments. I bought one there and then, a bowl that gives a low-pitched A, which I still love to this day. I just knew that this was my vocation.

It was the summer, as I remember, and the back door was open on to our sunny garden. Telsa was in and out of the sunshine. Lying sunbathing and getting too hot, then coming in to lie on the cool tiles in the kitchen.

I began to unpack my bowls and as I did, Telsa became curious. She watched as I put them on the floor. She hadn't seen crystal bowls before and she didn't know that they were to become a permanent fixture in our home.

I set them up and began to play about with them, listening to the different sounds they made. Telsa's ears pricked up and her head moved side to side as it always did when something was different or she could see spirits and angels. She darted back and forth, towards them and then away from them, not really knowing what to do with them. After a while she settled and sat down to listen to the music. I deliberately kept the volume down as animals have much more sensitive ears than we humans do. As I played and sang quietly, I think Telsa began to enjoy it; she lay down as if to listen properly. This made me realize that if Telsa could enjoy the sounds the bowls made, with her highly sensitive ears, less sensitive humans would definitely be able to enjoy it too.

I began to do evening sound workshops and would take Telsa along so people could see how the sound of the bowls and singing could affect their animals as well as people. It was a great success and I'm sure Telsa's calm response made people feel more comfortable about trying it.

That was the start of me moving further along my pathway doing something that I loved; and Telsa was moving along it with me.

I then began to do one-to-one sound healings with the bowls and one-day workshops, which Telsa very often attended.

At one sound workshop in the Midlands there were, I think, about eighteen people. Telsa walked around and greeted everyone in turn before we began. There was a woman there in a wheelchair, who had not walked for some years. Her sister had brought her to see how she would respond to the sound healing.

As I began to play, I noticed Telsa get up and sit on the woman's feet.

I had to carry on playing as everyone was in meditation. By this time I was used to Telsa going to wherever she felt right, but I was still always a bit apprehensive about what the client's reaction might be when they realized.

Twenty minutes later the meditation came to a close. I brought everyone back into the room and made sure they were all grounded and protected after the healing.

The next minute, the woman stood up – yes, stood up from her wheelchair – and rushed straight up to me, hugged me and said that she had felt lots of tingling in her feet and legs and just knew that she could walk again. We were all completely stunned at this amazing instant recovery and from that day forward I began not to worry and to leave Telsa to her own devices. She knew better than I what she should be doing.

In one sound workshop for healing, we were doing the usual sound meditation. Telsa at first sat beside a member of the group named Judith, then lay down on her feet as I played the crystal bowls about half an hour. After the healing Judith was so upset that I had to ask her if she was all right. She said she had a tumour on her brain and the doctors had said they didn't hold out much hope of her recovery even if they operated. She was faced with the terrifying decision as to whether to have the operation or not. She had come to the sound workshop as her last hope, and had felt a lot of tingling throughout her body, which she found overwhelming. The following week she went to her doctor and, to her and the doctor's amazement, and the doctor's inability to explain this, the tumour had shrunk and virtually disappeared.

Not long before Telsa passed over in 2009 she was so enjoying the singing bowls that she would sit in on absent sound healing sessions, which I would record onto CD and send to the client. She began to enjoy them too much, though, and would snore! I'm sure it was in tune with the sound but it was not what anyone had ordered or was expecting . . . I therefore had to start putting her in the other room, but I'm sure she heard and enjoyed the sound just the same.

A CD for
Animal Healing

In June 2008 I was attending a reunion for the Diana Cooper School in Findhorn. I travelled up to Aberdeen by air, with my special crystal bowls in my luggage.

At the bus station I discovered that I would have to change buses at Blackburn en route to Findhorn, and that the wait for the bus would be 45 minutes. However a kind driver who was going in that direction with only a couple of passengers offered to make a short detour to take me to Blackburn.

Gratefully, I boarded the bus with my suitcase and my cases of crystal bowls. At the end of the 20-minute journey to Blackburn, the driver helped me with my cases and then drove off. As the bus was disappearing over the hill I realized I had left my handbag on my seat, with my phone and money in it. I felt a panic coming over me but I started to do some deep breathing and asked the angels to help me.

Just then another bus came along, so I explained to the driver about my handbag and asked if he could contact the driver of the previous bus. He couldn't do anything immediately but said he would ask when he got back to the depot, and come back, which would take two hours. I had no choice but to trust and to wait. Unbelievably, though, a few minutes later the original bus reappeared. The driver had noticed my handbag on the seat and had done another detour to bring it back to me.

What an angel in disguise! I thanked the angels for this earth angel who had come to help me.

I arrived at Cluny College, Forres, where we were to stay. The sanctuary was lovely; empty and with no red light on, so I went in and started chanting and singing by myself. It was a beautiful peaceful room. I was enjoying my chanting when I felt a big whoosh of energy come into me as I saw a large pink and golden orb come forward from the wall towards me. As this was happening, my chanting changed to "Come on Eileen", an old pop hit from the 70s. I had no idea why I was singing it, but then a voice said "It's Eileen … Eileen Caddy – and we want you to make a recording with your crystal bowls in the sanctuary for an animal healing CD." I saw a brief vision of St Francis and that was it, they were gone. As he is the patron saint of animals, I just knew I should at least try to do this, but I hadn't a clue how it would work; I had no recording equipment, and it would take me at least 45 minutes to unpack and prepare my bowls and the same again to put them away afterwards, and this was a very busy place.

I had, funnily enough, already been thinking of recording an animal-healing CD. The vets who treated Telsa and had done the healing training with me had asked me to record one for their animal-healing sessions, and it had got me thinking.

Everyone arrived at the college then and we gathered for a meditation. Diana led it and I played the singing bowls. A group member, Rosalie came up to me and asked if I would mind if she recorded it. Wow, I thought, maybe there's the recorder for my CD.

Later in the weekend, I asked Rosalie if she would mind recording me singing with the crystal bowls if it could be arranged in the sanctuary. She was happy to do so if the staff would allow us the time and space.

I was leaving the next day; I just had to do it, or at least try!

I asked if I could book the sanctuary for a session, but it was not possible. I decided I would just have to chance someone else coming into the room and go for it!

Off Rosalie and I went to the sanctuary to unpack the bowls and set up. Rosalie set the recorder and off we went, asking the angels, masters, Telsa's energy and especially St Francis to be present. All was going well. I hadn't any idea of the time and Rosalie had moved into an altered state, so I had to guess when the time was up and lean over to switch off the recorder. Amazingly, just as I had finished packing up people started to come into the sanctuary – we had been given the exact time we needed to do the recording. It felt fantastic.

I tried the CD out on Telsa when I arrived home, and to my delight she lay down to meditate until it finished. That was another confirmation for me that this was the "right" healing for animals. Mission accomplished.

PART IV

Telsa and the Spirit World

The Crystal Skulls

In 2006 I attended one of Edwin Courtenay's Crystal Skull lectures and afterwards invited him to present at the first Celestial Light Healers event with Diana Cooper and myself the following year. I was so delighted for the three of us to be presenting together at Stoke-on-Trent, very close to my hometown; it felt very special for me there and be able to connect to my father through my music. Many people thought I was crazy, holding this first big event in a marquee in early March – basically still winter. Maybe I was, but it all seemed to work out, and the event, in Trentham Gardens, was marvellously successful.

This event was also very special because it was here that I was properly introduced to the crystal skulls and their consciousness, for which Edwin is a channel. I had already had the chance to handle one or two of the skulls and Edwin knew well that I was not keen on them and that I thought they had scary eye sockets.

Edwin had come to stay at my house in Newcastle and do two days of readings. He had brought Kaora Psephone with him, his bottle-green obsidian life-size contemporary crystal skull. After the day's readings, Edwin said that Kaora would like to stay overnight with me and would that be OK?

I agreed and asked him to leave her in the room where he was doing the readings.

Later that evening I decided to go and look at Kaora. I was taking no chances so I took Telsa with me; I knew that if Telsa thought Kaora was all right, that was good enough for me.

We went upstairs and I opened the door. Immediately Telsa sat in the doorway and moved her head from side to side. I knew something was going on but also knew it was OK. Telsa then went towards Kaora. She sat right in front of her and put her eyes right up to the eye sockets of the crystal skull. I was speechless and waited and watched for about two or three minutes until Telsa moved away and came back to me. Telsa had obviously been fine, so I decided to do the same. I went up to Kaora and placed my eyes next to her eye sockets, just as Telsa had done – and I had an amazing experience, just as Telsa must have had. I didn't quite understand all the information I was getting, but it was definitely lovely information and wonderful energy.

What Telsa did that evening with the crystal skull was to trust and accept, and show me how to trust and accept. She completely got rid of my fear, to the extent that soon afterwards I bought myself a crystal skull. Her name is Sophia and she is a medium-sized rose quartz skull. From being frightened of the crystal skulls, I have become someone who has my own – all thanks to Telsa!

Telsa

· · · ·

by Edwin Courtenay

Telsa, the "wonder dog" as I think of her, has to be one of the most unusual animals I have ever encountered in my entire existence. She had that rather disconcerting way of looking at you with a worldly-wise and weary way that gave the impression she had seen it all before, at least 100,000 times, and hadn't even been terribly impressed the first time around! She gazed at you with her deep dark bottomless eyes, and you could almost hear her thinking – "Ah poor thing, look at it, thinking it's all evolved and knowledgeable"! She had a powerful presence that radiated calm and ease, grace and love, and she never complained or whimpered, no matter how many of Rosemary's singing bowls fell on her in the back of the car; never seemed hyper or needlessly excitable – unless she was chasing after something Rosemary had thrown for her – and never seemed anything other than exceptional and special and uniquely different.

Telsa would stare with unblinking concentration at spirit people that otherwise only I could see, or "light up" with healing energy when she was around people in need, never making a fuss or (like we humans are all too prone to do) making sure that everyone was looking at her. Telsa would just get on with it, with a quiet dignity and naturalness which seemed, if anything, to make what she was doing all the more extraordinary.

Telsa was a wonder dog, no more and certainly no less.

Once, when attending an angelic reiki weekend with Rosemary, I was given the task of giving Telsa karmic healing. Going through all the usual motions, I was overwhelmed by a barrage of images of Telsa's many past lives. She had often been a dog but had also lived as other animals, often by Rosemary's side and always helping, healing, protecting and guiding those she had paired with. Not once during this process did I get the feeling that I was healing her – quite the opposite, she was healing me, and I became filled with brilliant golden energy and light that welled up through me like a fountain and out of the top of my head. When the healing session had finished Telsa rolled over and fell asleep with an almost audible "That was easy and not terribly interesting"! I was amazed by this. I had come into contact with "special" animals before and even been the guardian of a few, but I had never encountered one quite so special, quite so evolved.

Towards the end of Telsa's earthly life I observed her care and concern for Rosemary and her attempts to reassure her that everything would be all right and that she would never be far away from Rosemary's side. This would, I thought, be a courageous thing for any human to do and a very conscious thing at that – to know when one was on the threshold of passing. To see a dog so aware was really remarkable – for it was clear that she did indeed know – and I remember hoping that when my day comes I might have such dignity and foresight.

When she had passed, I witnessed her on many occasions accompanying Rosemary in workshops and at events, sitting – to my clairvoyant sight – as solidly as you or I at Rosemary's foot or curled up and asleep like she used to do in earthly life.

Sometimes she would show her more "cosmic" side and appear like a fairy dog of old made entirely from light, beaming her healing radiance to those in need. I'm glad to say I see her still and benefit from her still, as I continue to see her acting from spirit as Rosemary's aide and familiar.

In truth I don't know what Telsa was or is: an angel incarnated as an animal (I've known such things before); a highly evolved canine or some form of healing channel of intense light. What I do know for sure is that she was an old, old soul and that I was very honoured to have known her – this time around – for the very short time that I did. Telsa was and is a blessing and an inspiration to us all, a testament to the power of love and spirit and a presence to aspire to, a presence of great grace and beauty.

I complete then my little contribution to this homage by handing over to one greater than I – the ascended master Kuthumi – allowing spirit to speak a little about this marvellous creature, I hope my small attempt here to explain a little regarding Telsa has made a few of you smile and opened a few people's minds to the infinite possibility of our reality and those often ignored and unsung heroes who surround us all the time in the natural and domestic world. Here's to Telsa – the wonder dog.

KUTHUMI SAYS...

It has long been humanity's presumptuous folly to imagine that they are the most superior and evolved beings on the planet, gauging these things through the creations, inventions and discoveries that they have made. However, those on the spiritual path know that spirituality is not dependent upon academic knowledge or power, civilized behaviour or creative expression, but rather on demeanour and heart. One does not have to be learned to be spiritual, one does not even have to be able to speak or make others understand what you know.

Spirituality is not what one does: rather what one is, what one radiates – and animals have the power to shine in this way just as all other living things do. There is no doubt that Telsa is an exceptional being, was an exceptional dog or that she is one of many – some here and some in spirit – who have since the beginning of time worked for the light often unseen, unheard, unacknowledged but nonetheless as hardworking and effective (if not more so) than man is. Telsa was a harbinger of light, a spirit of healing and truth, grace and a being who could touch the very core, heart and spirit of a person with her disarming nature. She, like many others, advanced and still advances the positive evolutionary movement of the world. It is our hope, then, as it is her hope too, that this little book if nothing else alerts you, dear reader, to the possibility not only that you might not be the most spiritual being in the room, the most evolved and hardworking and knowing, but also that you might be alerted to the truth that the light of spirit burns all around you in creatures great and small and that the Divine can manifest as easily in a domestic dog as it can a priest or priestess. For the Divine is in all things and often chooses those who have no need of ego to do its greatest work. Be mindful then of this and in the future pay more attention to those animals that you meet; you might not only have known them before but they might be responsible for the continuation of the evolution of your soul.

Telsa and Auras

In my healing groups over the years, among the many things Telsa has come across and joined in with are healing and spiritual experiences to do with colour and auras.

One evening at my friend Kate's house in Madeley, Cheshire, we were talking over a day course I'd just run on colour and auras. Kate asked me if I could see an aura around her husband Paul, who was sitting on the settee with Telsa lying on his knee snuggled up to his left side. Both were fast asleep.

I looked over and to my surprise I could see a bright emerald-green ball of light, moving up and around from Telsa's body up the left-hand side of Paul's body. Telsa was healing Paul while he was asleep and I might never have noticed if Kate hadn't asked me that question.

We were both amazed, but we left them to get on with their healing session.

I noticed Telsa's bright emerald-green healing light again while I was staying in Tynemouth with my son and his father. Chris the black Labrador had not been well; she was thirteen years old after all and getting weary, and we were worried about her. Telsa lay by her and the emerald-green light began to move from her to Chris. Telsa was healing her. I'm sure she was helping Chris over to the spirit world, as the black Labrador died two days after Telsa and I had left to come back to Cheshire.

The next weekend I was running a two-day ascension class and, when we had finished our last meditation, I asked as usual if anyone had anything to share. One of the group members, Caroline, said "The strangest thing happened… it's a bit bizarre, but Telsa has been giving me healing! She lay on my left foot and I felt and saw the energy moving up my leg from my left foot – I know she was giving me healing." I knew that this had happened – I had seen the emerald-green light moving from Telsa to Caroline.

As well as this green light, a bright white light would sometimes surround Telsa, showing me again what a very powerful healer she was.

I was running a two-day Sounds of Ascension group in Cheshire, and Telsa was in attendance as always. One of the meditations, a powerful light-body activation, was in progress. Telsa was sitting in the room, but a little way apart, outside of the group. I asked the master Melchizedek, who was in biblical times a great spiritual teacher to Abraham, Moses and Noah, to place his rod of power into the crown chakra of each participant. Telsa suddenly moved into the centre of the group and as I saw the white light building up around her she swivelled round to each participant, gazing at each person intently. I could see that she was passing some information to each one in turn.

After another ascension workshop, where we had worked on attuning everyone and using the crystal bowls, one group member, Julia, asked for a photograph of all of us.

Telsa did not normally want to be in photos, but this day, strangely for her, she really did; I tried to move her away but she insisted on sitting in front of us for the picture.

When the picture came out, there was a huge, beautiful pink orb of love coming from Telsa and surrounding us all!

Mischievous Spirits and Lost Souls

When I moved away from Newcastle down to Cheshire in 2000, I bought a house in Alsager that needed complete renovation. Alsager was a village just a few miles away from my roots and my family. I was born in this area and I had moved here to have some peace and quiet after going through some very difficult experiences. I knew this place would be good for me; I wanted to get back to my roots, and hopefully connect with my dearly departed father.

I started working on renovating this quaint cottage, which I knew would need a lot of work and TLC to get it to feel right.

There were mischievous spirits and lost souls in this cottage, as we began to find out!

Telsa had always slept on the landing outside my bedroom, but in this cottage she didn't want to.

After we had been there a few weeks I started to notice the smell of fried onions, seemingly coming from upstairs – at the top of the landing. I just thought it was a coincidence at first, even though I wasn't cooking onions at the time, but I gradually realized that that must be why Telsa was not happy in that spot. I went to inspect it and could feel that there was a strange energy at the top of the stairs. I began to tune in to it and it turned out that it was a seemingly harmless old lady and a cook who had worked in the house a long time ago, when it was one large house. This lady hadn't been too keen on dogs, I could tell. I'm not sure what had happened to her but she was eventually glad to go with the angels to the light; the smell disappeared, the funny energy left and it made a big difference to the house, which Telsa and I could both feel.

I sometimes wonder if this was a training period for me to learn how to send lost souls to the light; these events carried on for a while, both at my cottage and at friends' houses.

For a while Telsa and I had to work with the spirits of many wartime pilots, who had been shot down or bombed and were still hanging around between dimensions, not really knowing where they were or how to get to the light.

In the evenings I would often see energy shapes appearing on the wall, of a pilot and an aeroplane, the pilot with his gas mask on. Very often I could even see the symbol on the plane and knew that sometimes the pilots were British and sometimes German. Telsa and I would call in Archangel Michael, the archangel of protection, to put his bubble of electric-blue light around us. I would ask Archangel Sandalphon to ground us and St Germain and Archangel Zadkiel to use the violet flame, which transmutes lower energies to higher. I would tune in to the pilots, talk to them and ask if they wanted to go to the light and they always did – that was what they had come for. I would surround them in white light and they would wave to me as they were taken by the angels to the light. I would watch Telsa and know she could see the spirits too. Many pilots, I discovered, had been bombed and killed in this area. There had been an ammunitions factory about a mile away during World War II, which had been a target for the Germans.

Similar things happened in other people's houses too; there are a lot of lost spirits trying or needing to get to the light. Telsa and I did our work but I didn't always tell the inhabitants of the house what we were doing. Some people might have thought we were crazy and been scared. Unless they were open to the spirit world and I knew they would understand and could handle it, I didn't say anything, just continued with this very rewarding work.

Once when I was away from home, singing with the Halle Choir in Warwick, I looked through the window of my bed-and-breakfast bedroom and saw in the field outside a vision of many uniformed soldiers, a gruesome and sad sight as many of them had severed heads, arms or legs. Their leader, or general, looked foreign, although I couldn't place his nationality. These visions would not go away for quite some time and I went downstairs for breakfast still wondering what it was all about.

As I was travelling home later, I put the radio on and heard that it was Remembrance Sunday, Poppy Day. My vision must have been about helping those souls who had been killed in that area to the light.

I got home and saw to my surprise that my Sunday newspaper had a picture on the front page of the same general I had seen in the field outside my window. It was Stalin.

Other Spirit Happenings

When Joe and I were still living in Tynemouth with Telsa, we had a lovely Victorian semi-detached house with loads of character. Joe was a teenager and wanting lots of pals round at the house, so we made the upstairs loft space into a bedroom-cum-lounge for him. Telsa was upset that she couldn't get up there to Joe and the boys, so I arranged to have a spindle staircase made specially for her so that she could get up there!

Occasionally there were goings-on up there, not only with the boys but with spirit beings – mischievous ones at that!

One evening Joe had gone to bed and he had no one sleeping over, so all was quiet upstairs. At 2 a.m. I heard loud music playing from Joe's room. I called to him to turn it down but there was no answer. I got up and went up to the loft – not too happy, I might add – and found Joe fast asleep with Telsa on his bed. I tried to wake him but couldn't, so I decided to leave it until morning and went back to bed, wondering what was going on.

The following morning I asked Joe why he had put his music on so loud in the middle of the night with no consideration for others, and he told me it was always happening. He would take the CDs out and unplug the machine but it still came on. Telsa and I investigated and discovered that Joe had company in the loft; the spirit of a woman who had lived in our house years earlier and had died suddenly there. She was obviously trying to catch our attention to help her...and she did. Telsa and I helped this spirit to the light and we were all able to sleep soundly again.

After Joe's father had passed, in 2005, we were living in his house. In the kitchen was a green kettle, an old-fashioned one that whistled, which he'd always claimed he bought by "accident". We used to tease him about it, saying that we couldn't believe he would buy something with such an awful whistle. It was really loud and it always made us laugh.

After he had passed over that kettle used to switch itself on many times a day and whistle loudly and annoyingly. Telsa would come into the kitchen moving her head from side to side and wagging her tail. She could see what was going on. We knew it was Joe's dad letting us know he was around and that he too could see the funny side of the whistling kettle now!

Past Lives with Telsa

Telsa and I and also my son Joe have had many past-life experiences together. Some of these have been revealed in the angelic past-life healing I have done when training my groups.

There was one particular day in Stoke-on-Trent. We were an odd number on the course, so I used Telsa as a client, and group member Julia partnered Telsa in a past-life healing session. Here is Julia's experience in her own words…

> Telsa was showing me that we had known each other as energy beings in Lemuria, in the old pre-Atlantean civilization. Telsa had a very high energy and she told me that she had enjoyed incarnating as an animal over many lifetimes as she felt she could do more healing in that form without making a fuss; people just accepted her love and healing without question. I also saw Telsa healing the Earth. She was a very wise being and I felt honoured to be in the presence of such a highly evolved soul.

In another workshop I decided to do a past-life healing on Telsa myself.

Telsa appeared as a black cougar with a beautiful shiny coat and a glittering jewelled collar. She was the prince's pet in Shah Jhan's palace at Agra, next to the Taj Mahal. Joe was also living here at this time, as the prince of the palace. They, Joe and Telsa, were with Lord Kuthumi (Shah Jhan) in the palace. Telsa in her lifetime as my dog had an amazingly bright, glossy coat, right up to her passing. Many people used to remark on how shiny her coat was.

I have had confirmation on this through a recent reading with Doreen, a clairvoyant and friend in Newcastle: she said, "There is a beautiful shiny black cougar very close to your son, guiding him." That made so much sense to me, as Telsa had passed to spirit by then, and I had already seen her in a past life as a beautiful glossy cougar.

In another past life Telsa was a human, a quiet, wise, prophetic old man with a white beard: a healer. He was looked upon very favourably in his community and many people went to him for spiritual guidance.

In a past life in Atlantis, Telsa partnered Joe and me many times as we did our work as healers. We made up a trio that was to be together over a number of lifetimes in Atlantis.

CAROLINE

In March 2007 I was attending Rosemary's angelic reiki masters course. Telsa had decided that I should have a new experience and would not be dissuaded from lying by my chair. Rosemary moved her away, but she was determined to return. I sat down and Telsa linked in with my energy, with her left paw on my left foot. As Telsa started her channelling, I felt very emotional and was aware of an amazing energy. Everyone else was having a 4th-degree clearing meditation but I was experiencing a trip in a spaceship to Sirius with Telsa! Sirius was orange and barren and people were busy; spaceships were plentiful. One particular spaceship was circulating around Sirius, and bands of colour also spun around the planet. Telsa and I went into an important building where I was told that she had come to Earth as a dog this time as it would be easier for her to move around people and offer healing than to come here in human form. She and I were both on Earth to heal.

I then saw a larger spacecraft and Rosemary, Telsa and I merged as one huge ball of bright white energy.

At the entrance to the spaceship Diana Cooper was present with us. Hundreds of people were boarding the ship; we had all undertaken a soul contract to do this work. I was also told that we needed to visit Luxor in Egypt, Macchu Picchu and Mexico to link this energy to make a connected power grid, and that it was very important for the earth that we do this.

Telsa moved her paw off my foot, walked away and my amazing experience ended.

I had tears running down my cheeks, but I was not crying for myself or out of sadness; it was the emotion from my soul reconnecting with home.

Synchronicities

When Telsa was five years old, I noticed a lump on her head. I took her to the vet and they said it seemed to be all right but if it got any larger to come back and they would do a biopsy. I just knew it needed seeing to, so went back to the vet two days later and asked for the biopsy. They did it there and then, sent the sample away and phoned me the next day. I remember how I felt when the vet said she had a malignant tumour on the top of her head. I immediately arranged for an operation and started doing healing on her several times a day. The vets operated and said they had done all they could and the rest was up to Telsa. We kept the healing going for another week, then went back for a check-up to see how she was doing. They had removed the tumour and surrounding areas and could not assure me it would not return. We never stopped doing the healing, and by now I had met the vets at Croft, who began treating her with homeopathic medicine. I really think that treatment and the healing did the trick. She was cleared of the cancer and it only recurred about a month before she passed over. How blessed I was to have her for another six years – for the most important years in both mine and Telsa's life.

~

It was 2000 and I had moved to Alsager just a few months ago. I was asleep in bed and Telsa was sleeping on the landing in her bed. My bedroom door was open, and I had felt Telsa jump onto my bed, which was very unusual – she knew I liked my own space in bed. Within a short space of time the central light-fitting on the ceiling started to sway and shake, so much that I could hear the glass rattling. The wall lights over my headboard also began to shake and I had to hold on to them in case they shattered over me. Then the bed began to shake. The whole house began vibrating and shaking. I remember thinking that surely there must be some massive articulated truck going past my cottage! It stopped after a couple of minutes and all went back to normal. I eventually went back to sleep, quite bewildered and wondering whatever could have caused this tremor, and so did Telsa I'm sure.

About 7 a.m. the following morning a friend phoned me, saying "did the earth move for you?". Apparently there had been an earthquake south of my village; it had been on the news and had caused much damage in the area. I then realized that Telsa had sensed this earthquake before it reached our house and came to lie on my bed, very unusually for her, to protect both of us.

~

Telsa and I were attending a spiritual mediumship circle in Newcastle upon Tyne, where I had been asked to play my crystal bowls and sing.

I felt that there was some very intensive karmic healing going on. This was confirmed when I saw a ball of bright white light building up on and around Telsa.

I could feel and see the angelic and masters' energies, building and becoming more and more intense. I did not feel the need to go into detail with the group about this deep healing as I knew spirit was taking the opportunity to do healing as well as mediumship on this occasion.

That evening, thinking back to the day, I realized there had been two people in the group needing some very deep healing and Telsa and I had been there to facilitate this.

When I went to bed Telsa again got up onto the bed, which was unusual. Suddenly two dragonlike creatures appeared and began hissing at Telsa and me. I realized that these were the lower entities from the two people and that they needed to be sent to the light. Telsa held the light while I did the healing and clearing with the angels. I was so fortunate to have her with me; she had so much strength and I really needed it for this difficult task.

PART V

Working from
the Other Side

Telsa Ascends

On 6 May 2009 Joe and I realized Telsa was not well. Joe tried to avoid the issue; it was so painful for him. I tried to accept the fact that she was tired now and knew her days were numbered, but part of me did not want to believe this either. The vet had X-rayed her and couldn't see anything, but we knew there was something wrong with her. Joe could see that Telsa was not herself and I was trying to prepare myself for the hardest moment I would have to face.

Joe came round to my house in the afternoon for a chat, and Telsa, unusually for her, lay in his arms the whole time. He held her for well over an hour but eventually had to go home. Telsa really didn't want him to go. She knew this was to be her last time with Joe and she wanted to make the most of it.

In the evening she began to get very restless and was obviously not happy. I knew I would have to take her to the emergency vet in Gateshead as it was 11.30 p.m. now. I rang Joe, but his phone was off. I went round to his house, but there was no answer. I found out later that he had been asleep, which with hindsight was how it had to be; Telsa had said her goodbyes to Joe in the afternoon, and obviously he didn't need to be put through this next trauma.

I gently helped Telsa into the back of the car, cuddling her and telling her she would be all right. She was crying, which was very upsetting. I knew she was hurting and that there was nothing that I could do for her now.

I was so upset that I had to ask the angels to help me find the surgery, as this was not the practice I usually took Telsa to. I eventually arrived in Gateshead and had a wonderful surprise to see the staff there. They looked to me like five angelic beings; all youngish women and so lovely.

As the vet checked Telsa's temperature, a tumour burst, a tumour no one had known about. I thank God that it waited until I arrived at the vets. We knew it was time for Telsa to go but it was incredibly hard for me to accept. The vets gave Telsa a sedative and kindly allowed me to sit in the room with her for a few minutes on our own. I couldn't believe it; my worst fear, of losing my best friend and healing partner, was happening. I talked to her, in a daze but thanking her for being with me and being my healing partner. Then I cuddled her, and then I told the vet I was ready. She gave Telsa the injection to put her to sleep as I held her.

I will never forget those last few moments when she slowly went heavy in my arms. Just as she went, there on the wall appeared a huge ball of the bright emerald-green light of Archangel Raphael, surrounded by golden-hued white light. I knew then that her soul had definitely gone straight to the light to be with the masters and angels.

Telsa, as I had known her, passed peacefully away just after midnight on 7 May 2009. My life was going to change dramatically overnight. I felt sick, lonely and angry. Every emotion you can imagine was welling up in me. Even though I knew Telsa had not really died, that she would live on in spirit, I would still have to go through the physical loss of not having her around me at home and in my healing groups.

I tried to tell myself it would all work out the right way and it was meant to be – and eventually, in fact, it has.

Telsa will always be in my life through my healing, and for that I am truly grateful.

Her visual calling card is the bright emerald-green light surrounded by golden white light, which often appears to me when I am doing a healing and feel in need of Telsa's particular energy.

Telsa is working with the ascended master Kuthumi, who was also St Francis of Assisi. It doesn't surprise me at all that Telsa is working with St Francis to heal other members of the animal kingdom; she loved other dogs, and cats and other animals, very much when she was alive with me.

I had made a strong connection to St Francis three years ago, when I went to visit Assisi. I was singing in Rome and decided to go on a day trip with my singer friend Alice. I knew I had a connection to this master, so I was very eager to tread his path in Assisi.

We had only three hours to see the whole of the town. I decided to go with the flow and allow the best places and churches to come to me; it would be impossible for us to see all of them.

The first church we came across was the imposing main church of St Francis, with beautiful murals by the artist Giotto. After this we walked to a very small unmarked church, which was pulling me inside it. No objets d'art in here, only a tiny window, a font and a few rows of wooden seats. I went inside and stood in the aisle near the small window, which allowed a beam of bright light to enter and strike where the altar would have been. I was rooted to the spot. It was like a bolt of lightning and electricity flashing through me. I knew that this was a very powerful spot, and when I bought a guidebook later I learned that this was the place where St Francis was born and where he spent most of his years teaching.

I had received my connection and we were both well pleased with our visit to Assisi.

One of the past-life incarnations of the ascended master Kuthumi, as I've said, is St Francis of Assisi. Other past lives of this master are Shah Jhan, who built the Taj Mahal in Agra, India in memory of his dearly beloved wife, and Pythagoras, who gave humankind his work on sacred geometry, the music of the spheres and mathematics.

Kuthumi was Balthazar, one of the Bible's wise men, and Tuthmosis III, pharaoh of Egypt. He was also a founder member of the Knights Templar, who kept ancient esoteric secrets and protected the pilgrims.

Telsa is also working with Archangel Raphael.

Archangel Raphael is the angel of healing, abundance, creativity, truth and the ability to see with the third eye. Raphael helps you concentrate and focus and enhances your ability to create through visualization. His twin flame is Mother Mary, mother of Jesus, also known as the Queen of Angels.

Archangel Raphael works on the emerald-green ray of the heart, the beautiful light that was present when Telsa passed over.

TELSA MY DEAREST FRIEND
from Rosemary

You were always full of fun
Always there to get things done
I am learning to go it alone
Finding solace in my new home
Knowing you're there helps me so
For you're always with me I really know
Eager to help, eager to heal
Making people happy
So dedicated it's unreal

All connections you made so well
Working with other healers as well
Telsa, my love, you deserve all your light
I learnt a lot, from your insight
I'm sure you're doing a good job now
With all the others there somehow
Making people smile and laugh
Carrying the healing staff
Go for it girl… I feel so proud
When my time comes, I'll shout out loud
Telsa, Telsa, we meet again
I know that things will be the same.

After Telsa's Passing

Immediately after Telsa's passing Edwin Courtenay emailed me with beautiful news: had this message from Kuthumi last night…

MESSAGE FROM KUTHUMI

Telsa is with me now adjusting to her new state in my care. She is eager to return to you and has been given special dispensation to continue to do so as your totem animal and familiar spirit because she is so special and so are you. She will visit with me this weekend after which she will return to spirit for a little while before returning to you to continue your healing work together.

Know that all is how it was meant to be and that you did what was for the greater good of all.

You are greatly loved, dearest Rosemary.

Yours, *Kuthumi*

This message was SO comforting and helped me immensely in getting through this very challenging time.

Telsa now comes to visit me regularly, her big soft brown eyes gazing at me and a bright emerald-green ball of light, or as a brilliant-green dog shape or sometimes in the shape of a bone. I am so blessed to be able to acknowledge her and know that she is still around. She still works with me in my groups, holding the light and healing where necessary.

She wants to work with all the members of my groups who she met and worked with during her lifetime. She will let you know she is there. Just call her in. You will know.

In Hawaii

It was March 2009 and I had decided to go to Hawaii, taking my crystal singing bowls as always when I travelled. Eventually I got a group together, all keen to visit this very spiritual place.

We started in Kuwaii, for me the most spiritual of the islands, where we managed to see the Earth Keeper Crystal, which is housed in a glass cabinet in the Hindu temple.

After a few days we travelled to the main island, the largest and probably the most commercialized. After that beautiful energy on Kuwaii, the energy here felt completely different, so I decided that this was the time to just have a holiday. The hotel was beautiful and jutted out over the bay, making it feel as though we were on a boat on the water.

My group had booked a full-day trip out to see and swim with the dolphins. Setting off to sea after a lovely, short meditation, we looked back and saw the most wonderful cloud formation and all felt that something powerful was going to happen today.

The captain spotted some dolphins leaping in and out of the water in the distance, so we headed out to them. We all had snorkels and flippers, but no lifejackets. I had completely forgotten that I was not a good swimmer and just went along with the rest, into the water.

As I started to climb down the boat ladder, though, I started to panic and decided I couldn't let go. I told everyone to go ahead and I would look after the boat. I began to feel a little upset and vulnerable, really wanting to go out with the dolphins but not being brave enough. Just then I felt a massive presence with me. It was Telsa; she had obviously heard my call and felt my panic, and come to my aid. She stayed close by me and I started to feel much better. I started singing under the water and asked the dolphins to please meet me halfway as I couldn't do any more.

I closed my eyes and to my surprise I saw a humpback whale swimming towards me. I thought this was a bit strange as I had been talking to the dolphins, and as no one had mentioned whales, I just kept on singing.

The captain came back a few minutes later and persuaded me to hold on to her so she could take me around the water to see the coral. It was beautiful and I started to feel much better.

Everyone boarded again and off we went out to sea even further.

Again we spotted some humpback whales, on their way to Alaska to feed after breeding in Hawaii.

The two whales seemed to be swimming towards us, just as the one had while I was meditating in the water. One of the whales kept swimming and came right up to our boat, under and out the other side. My heart almost seemed to jump out of my body as the whale looked me in the eye. I was overwhelmed and burst into tears. I said a special thank you to it, feeling sure that this was the whale I had connected with earlier. One of the most magical experiences of my life.

Telsa had once again helped me, by gently allowing me to recover from the fear and panic of being in the middle of the ocean and enabling me to be calm enough to sing and meditate and see that wonderful whale coming towards me. Thank you once again, Telsa.

Telsa is Working from Spirit

My healing has taken another turn now Telsa has passed. I am so truly blessed to still have contact with her whenever I ask, or when she feels it is the right time for her to be here in this world with me.

I missed Telsa so much that I moved house and area. I needed to be in a new space. A new start to carry on with my healing work for spirit.

I live in Bedale, North Yorkshire now, where I have started anew. I love it here and it has helped to change my life. Nothing stays the same forever.

In August 2009 I was running an angelic reiki course at Hazeldean in Carlisle. Some of the people on this course hadn't met Telsa and didn't know anything about her or her work.

We had just finished a meditation when a course member, Karen, said she was aware of a dark-coloured dog by my feet. That was wonderful confirmation for me, and quite a surprise for Karen when I told her about Telsa.

Telsa is particularly likely to visit my groups when she knows some of the people attending. She comes as a large brilliant emerald-green doggy shape, or in the shape of a bone, or she comes right up to my face and eyeballs me. I feel this very strong powerful energy when she is around, and I am so blessed to have that connection with her.

As I am writing this chapter Telsa has just struck one of my crystal bowls to play; I can feel her presence very strongly. She obviously wants to be part of this book, and who can blame her when she's the star!

I have attended residential mediumship weekends for a few years now at the Lindum in Lytham St Annes, where I usually do a sound workshop and meditation. Telsa has been in the workshops with me many times over the years. My fellow workshop members Kate and Caroline and I usually had adjoining rooms, Kate and Caroline in one room and me in the other, and Telsa used to sleep in the room with me.

Telsa always loved being part of this group and would join in the healing circles while I played my crystal bowls. The three of us were attending a weekend in November 2009, my first of these courses since her passing, and Telsa, in spirit, entered into the room, jumping around, so excited to be with us all again. Little did I realize that Telsa hadn't just come to be with us but that this was to be another working weekend for her.

I had arranged to do a karmic clearing/healing for Caroline, and we had decided that we would do it on the Sunday evening.

On Saturday we had been watching *X Factor* on the TV and couldn't be bothered to go downstairs again. I had been talking about one of the contestants, who had previously sung a brilliant version of "Purple Rain". We all sang this song for ages and couldn't get it out of our minds.

As Caroline, Kate and I lay on our beds talking, I suddenly felt two very powerful energies and saw a huge rose-pink light come in over Caroline, who began to feel its effects. It was Quan Yin, a female Chinese Ascended Master full of love and compassion.

The second powerful energy was Telsa, who I knew from her emerald-green Light and her presence. The healing was starting and we had to go with the flow. I could see and feel the loving light coming in around Caroline from Quan Yin, who was facilitating the healing with Telsa holding the light. I told Caroline that this was happening and that it looked as though the karmic healing was starting. I could see the rose-pink light now coming over Caroline in intermittent waves, and I could feel it myself too. Quan Yin was pouring unconditional love into this karmic situation, which was having its profound clearing effect on the lower energy that needed clearing. Caroline continues the story…

CAROLINE

As the healing was starting I saw a white light streaming through Rosemary's crown chakra, and was aware of a build-up of pink energy, the energy of Quan Yin, to my left, in front of me, by the adjoining door. Between the two bedrooms was a sharp green energy, which I knew was Telsa and which appeared in the shape of a bone.

The pink energy was building, now coming in waves every 2 or 3 minutes. A huge wave came through my left side and passed through me, leaving via my right-hand side. The energy reminded me of the first stages of childbirth! Rosemary could also feel and see this loving energy; she told me that it was filled with love.

The intermittent waves of energy began to subside after about 30 minutes and we thought the healing had finished for now. We both went to bed, but Rosemary suddenly started to feel the energy building again, and was aware of Telsa's presence.

Then I began to feel the discomfort of the childbirth-like waves of energy starting up again.

Rosemary had called in St Germain with the violet

flame, as well as the beings of light. Kate at that moment saw what she described as "purple rain" in the room, which then turned into a solid purple triangle and which confirmed to us that St Germain was here and assisting.

I then saw my karmic clearing and it looked like a creature from Greek mythology – not human, mammal nor fish. I felt it clear from my stomach and chest area as Rosemary held the energy at my legs, filling the room with pinkish-white and purple light.

I felt the need to send love to this creature and was aware of Archangel Michael cutting a large cord, like a bicycle inner tube, to release it from me.

I felt calm when this "operation" was over and went to sleep feeling that there had been a great release. I truly thank you, Telsa once again, for coming to be present at this deep clearing and healing."

In February 2010 I was taking an angelic healing group and the members were all practising healing on each other. One member, Noreen, who was working on healing Angie, saw her skirt wafting around her feet as if in a draught; she thought this was quite odd as the door and the windows were closed.

Angie told us afterwards that she had been aware of a dark-coloured dog sitting at her feet, pulling at her skirt. None of these students had known Telsa, so I hadn't mentioned this, but I had known that Telsa had been in the room healing along with us all!

From Sara Tazewell Scott

Sara has trained with Telsa and me in angelic reiki groups.

TELSA
...Gone but not forgotten

Telsa and Rosemary... what a pair
An awesome duo... healing gurus
One a natural... the other, well you'd never have guessed
Chalk and cheese, bubble and squeak
The healing energy just flowed without effort
She'd cover you with kisses
Because she knew you needed them
She knew what you needed
All you had to do was relax

She fell apart when the other one left
She needed warmth and cuddles
And still she can heal from where she is now
Up there, in the sky, betwixt the angels and St Francis.
Where she now belongs
She watches from afar
She helps her Master, her mate
As she helped me that day
When I needed a hug, a cuddle.
She leaps, she soars, she chases cats
She barks at nothing
Just like she used to
She nods, she pants, she gets up
She lies down, she tosses and turns

Until she gets comfortable
She sighs, she frets no more
For where she is, there is no need to sigh or fret
Everything is peaceful
Everything is healed

And so to work she goes
Her paws, her tongue is all she needs to heal
For she is the Healing dog
The wonder dog
Who knows you and what you need

So why has she gone
Where has she gone
Nowhere!!!
She is still here.
In mind and spirit
She hugs and cuddles still
She left to help you from afar
Without the need for physical presence
To help lighten your load
To help you heal more people but from afar
Now she's like a star!
Sparkling in the distance

Follow your heart, Rosemary
Let it lead you
Let it send you to promised lands
To feel the love, the security
The space,
The togetherness

The connectedness
Release me, release my body
There is a space, a place for you
Not here
Not now
Not ever
Not now in this lifetime
But together you will be once more
That time is now
That time is here
Connect to your heart
Telsa is guiding you
Ask for direction not
Just follow her paws
Her whispering in your ear
Follow her barks
Her muffled voice
For she is guiding you
Each and every one of you
Fear not you are not mad
It is voices you hear
It is that of a loved one
A spirit close at hand

There to help
To guide you on through difficult times
As well as the joyful happy ones

She muddles on she fears
Her eyes full of tears
How can she go on

They were a team
How can she heal
And be herself without her
She can, she knows she can
On a good day
But when the sky is black
The clouds abound
It is a little harder
To forget her dear departed friend
But she knows so well
She knows how it is
She knows where she is
She can feel her drawing near
But she forgets
It's harder when she's low
So healing to you my friend
To help you at this time
To stay with joy and wonder
The bird reminds me
As it hunts for seed on the path
Dropped by its mate when eating
That often we gain the most
From what seems at the time, a loss, a wrench
An earth-shattering event
Not to most
But to me and you

But we know she is near
Now and forever
God Bless you Telsa
May the Angels surround you

With healing light
Now and when you are at your lowest

Follow your heart
Like a breath to a new born child
A feather to a bird
A wing to a dove
A petal to a flower
A stream to a brook
And a river to an ocean
May your heart be filled
With laughter and joy
And tears of happiness
May your life be filled with love
And meaning once more
And may you flourish
And reach new heights
With her by your side.
Guiding you
From not so afar
Feel her there
Feel her touch
Feel her energy
Feel her be
In the blink of an eye
She is gone
But not for long
For she'll be back
To tickle your fancy
To stroke your hair
To lick your face

To warm your heart
To fill you up to overflowing
With pride and joy

Well, they didn't call me the wonder dog for nothing
Telsa… gone?… I'm not gone!
I'm just getting started.

With love and light
Sara Tazewell Scott

Enter Carna 2009

Following Telsa's passing and, shortly after, the passing of his best friend Lewis, my son Joe decided he needed a new puppy to help him through all the grieving.

Carna is a tan-coloured Dogue de Bordeaux French Mastiff, and she is absolutely gorgeous. She is a real handful but has helped fill the gap made by Telsa's passing. She has one of Telsa's old beds, and strangely she becomes very calm when she sits or lies in it. I have had to ask for Telsa's help many times when Carna has been naughty, and have seen and felt Telsa's energy come in and sit with Carna to calm her down.

Carna sings and howls just like Spot, the Staffordshire bull terrier my family had when I was young. We were a very musical family, as I've spoken of; for the choirs and the music which my grandfather, cousins and uncles always practised at our house for the brass band and choirs they were involved with.

Spot used to love it and would howl and sing along, especially to the brass instruments and when my father played the piano and sang. It is very funny now, years later, to hear Carna singing along to my music just like Spot used to.

Carna is another very tuned-in dog. Hopefully as she gets older and calms down I will be able to take her to some of my healing groups – although I think she will need some lessons from Telsa first!

One day over the Christmas period Lyndsey, Joe's partner, was lying on the settee with Telsa's favourite blanket over her and Carna lying on the floor near her. I saw Telsa, taking that now familiar green dog shape and giving off massive amounts of her energy, suddenly appear on the settee lying with Lyndsey on her old favourite blanket. Lyndsey could feel a heaviness and energy on her too, and was not at all surprised when I told her Telsa was with her.

I was talking to Joe about Telsa one day when Carna was about five months old. As we were chatting Joe drew my attention to the hair on Carna's back. It looked the same as Telsa's had; both had that distinctive "S" shape along their back. What a revelation this was! We had never seen this hair pattern in any other boxer than Telsa, and we'd never known any Dogue de Bordeaux to have one before either. I felt very strongly that this was confirmation from the ascended master Kuthumi that an aspect of Telsa's soul wanted to be with us again; this time, as she was Joe's dog, to swap roles and be with him full-time and me part-time. She has come to help heal Joe, with a completely different energy, personality and set of challenges to those that Telsa brought. In this incarnation she is hard work for Joe and very demanding and challenging, but of course gorgeous.

God bless you Telsa and Carna, we love you.

Arctic Experience

In February 2010, Diana Cooper and I went on an adventure to the Arctic circle, the Stellar Gateway Chakra of the planet. What an amazing trip. We slept one night in an igloo. We went snowmobiling through the night forest with a team of huskies to see the northern lights. This trip was the most incredible of all our Arctic adventures.

It was 10 p.m. and our group, eight of us in all, set off to the husky farm where our trip was to begin. It was a magical evening as always in the Arctic, nothing but glistening moonlit snow and bright, clear sky. I was particularly excited about this trip as, obviously, I love dogs and it was only a few months since I had lost Telsa.

There were four sleds, with six huskies to each one. I lay in the sled and Diana stood on the runners behind, positioned so she could use the brake if necessary. We were led out into the night forest by our trip leader on a snowmobile. Diana and I were the first sled in line and the others followed on. The snowmobile was the only light we had, so we stayed very close.

Our leader stopped and told us that as there was a reindeer herd ahead of us we would take a left turn to avoid them. Off we went in the beautiful night; the snow and ice were magical, with the stars shining like a net of Christmas lights above us in the clear sky.

Our leader took the planned sharp turn left, but our huskies didn't follow her and continued straight on. Diana tried to brake but the ice and snow were packed in the mechanism and the brake would not work. Eventually Diana somehow managed to ground us to a halt. Our leader came over on her snowmobile, shouting in alarm that we were in grave danger and were likely to sink at any moment. We were on a lake and on thin ice. Her snowmobile began to sink into the ice and she abandoned it and scrambled over to us on foot. Even in the darkness we could see the water starting to flood over the ice.

The huskies were howling, very stressed and anxious because their owner was shouting and screaming at all of us. We knew we had to calm them down or they would bolt out over the lake and into the dark forest. Just at that moment I felt an overwhelming presence and saw Telsa join the huskies. One of the dogs immediately lay down, and the rest became quiet and calm.

We knew that if we could keep the dogs and the owner calm we would have a chance of getting off the lake. Telsa came to join me in the sled, and all six huskies followed her and jumped on top of me. I was loving this experience and temporarily forgot about the danger; but Diana could still hear the ice cracking below us.

Our leader was furious and chased the dogs out of the sled. She told me to get out while we turned the sled round, but as I did my leg went through the ice and I think we all realized then exactly how much danger we were in.

Telsa was determined to get us off the lake, though, and she led the huskies, who followed her, turning quickly and racing off the ice, bumping into the other sleds on the way. Our group's other huskies and sleds followed in close pursuit.

The leader's snowmobile had completely disappeared under the ice by now and she had jumped on to one of the sleds. We had no lights now that the snowmobile was gone, and could see just one light, way in the far distance, which we headed for.

We all arrived back at 1 o'clock in the morning, safe but in shock at what had happened and aware of how lucky we were to be alive.

Telsa is obviously still determined to work for spirit and humans, even though she has passed over.

She saved us all again on this Arctic trip; it truly was the adventure of a lifetime, but not one to be repeated!

My Personal Healing

In 2010 I was beginning to struggle with my right leg and hip. By April I knew I needed to see a doctor. I thought I had probably badly pulled a muscle and it was taking rather a long time to heal. I could occasionally hear some cracking and crunching, too, but thought that was probably because of an old accident.

The G.P. examined me and sent me for an X-ray, and when the results came back I was shocked to hear that it was severe osteo-arthritis of the hip and that I could do with having a hip replacement this year. I didn't agree to meeting a consultant and having the operation immediately, but I eventually had to accept the fact that I needed it. My hip had got much worse and by the time of my appointment with the consultant I could barely walk – I had to use a stick – and I was in a lot of pain.

I hadn't slept for weeks and was completely exhausted. I had cancelled all my recent workshops and healing sessions as by now I had given in to taking medication for the pain. I couldn't take it for very long, though, as it made me feel very disorientated and nauseated.

I was at such a low ebb that I cried out to the angels for help. At that point, Telsa appeared to me from spirit. I was in so much pain, and so exhausted, that I hadn't thought of asking her or anyone else to come and help, but I was so relieved when she did. As a healer I have always told people to ask the angels for help when they need it, and now here I was in this dreadful situation and I had forgotten to ask the angels for myself!

Every night for a week Telsa would get on to my bed to give me healing. I could feel the weight of her body and see that familiar emerald-green light. During her appearances she showed me situations in my life that I needed to change and let go of, because they were blocking my energy. I was also on a mission to find a way of getting myself better and free from pain and the need for medication. Telsa helped me to recognize many things about myself, and after that week she did not come back to me for a while. She had done all she needed to do for now: the rest was up to me.

After Telsa's visits I began taking rosehip and glucosamine and performing sound healing on myself. Within just one week I was feeling much better. After two weeks I was almost completely pain-free and walking more normally, but going very carefully so I didn't knock myself back again. Many wonderful friends sent me healing too, and I send grateful thanks to all of them.

In October the date for my operation arrived. I was feeling much better by now – I'd even managed to move house! By this time I was beginning to wonder why I was having the operation.

I took a violet flame spray to spray on my bed and around the area to clear any lingering lower energies. The nurse asked me what the lovely smell was and, as I didn't feel that I should go into much detail, I said it was lavender to help me sleep, which was true to an extent. She asked me to spray it all round the ward so everyone would get a good night's sleep, which I was very happy to do. The nursing staff was very helpful and kind but kept asking if I wanted pain-relief medication. When I said I wasn't in pain and didn't need pain relief, they asked me what level of pain I was in on a scale of 1–10, and I was able to say truthfully about 1. I was beginning to feel I shouldn't be there at all!

The following morning, 18 October, I was waiting on my bed in my theatre gown, all prepared for the trolley to theatre, when the anaesthetist arrived to tell me he was going to give me an injection at the base of my spine. I was shocked as I had arranged for a general anaesthetic; but when I insisted on this he just said "Don't worry, you will be fine," and patted me rather patronizingly on the shoulder. At this point I recognized him; I had seen him, in a past life of his, in a German hospital during the war. I recognized his false smile and his eyes that were not smiling. I had discovered when I "met" him before that he had been party to operations performed without anaesthetic. I believe that he and I had had to meet to dissolve and clear in this lifetime the energy from that past life. I started to panic, and asked the angels to calm me down and help me. Within fifteen minutes the consultant came to tell me my operation had been cancelled as the person before me had taken longer than they had expected and there wouldn't be time for my operation. I couldn't believe it! I quickly got dressed and the staff called a taxi for me.

I had asked the angels to help with my situation and they had! When the hospital called to give me another date, two weeks later, I said I wasn't ready for the operation. I had to work on forgiveness for the anaesthetist and for myself to clear our past connection.

For the next couple of months I worked very hard trying to recover and treat this situation myself, and when I saw the consultant again on 10 December he could see how much better I was and said he couldn't believe how well I was moving about; I had no stick and was pain-free. He asked me about the healing and what I was taking, then he told me to just keep doing what I was doing and if I needed him in the future, just to contact the GP again.

I felt that an operation was not the right thing for me at that time, so I booked a Mediterranean cruise instead and I think that did me far more good! All the healing work I did on myself had paid off, facilitated as it was by the angels and, of course, by Telsa.

The Blizzard

As mentioned previously, I have recently moved to just outside the beautiful market town of Bedale on the edge of the Yorkshire Dales.

As you will no doubt remember, the heavy snowfalls and ice in the winter of 2010 made it a very challenging time for people in many parts of the country.

It was the beginning of December and I had decided that the roads were clear enough to go into Bedale for some shopping. As I was returning home something urged me to go into Richmond to collect a parcel I was waiting for. The roads seemed clear enough, so I decided to make the journey.

I had been driving for about ten minutes when suddenly the weather changed. A snow blizzard had set in. It was as though I had walked through the wardrobe to Narnia: I couldn't see my hand in front of me. I felt a bit apprehensive but carried on, thinking and hoping that this bad weather was just a pocket. No such luck! The roads were treacherous and there didn't seem to be anyone else about. I slowly drove up the hill to Scotton and, driving over the top, I saw a people-carrier in front of me in desperate trouble. It was spinning, skidding and sliding on the thick snow and ice on the road. As I was going downhill I was obviously gathering speed, and was trying not to use my brakes or I could easily end up colliding with this vehicle. I could now see that there were more cars, slowly making their way up the hill on the other side of the road. Oh my goodness, I thought. In a flash, a bright blue light appeared in front of me and the familiar emerald-green dog shape appeared on my front passenger seat. I felt all of a sudden very calm, and pulled well over to the other side of the road to try to avoid the spinning car, mounted the embankment and quickly pulled back over to the left side of the road and into the left-hand lane again just before I met the oncoming traffic. There were abandoned cars everywhere. It happened so quickly that I didn't have time to be afraid; it was only when I had come to a stop again, because of the stuck traffic surrounding the roundabout, that I realized I could have been caught up in a very nasty accident. I was glad to stop to get my breath, realizing what I had just avoided, once again with the help of Archangel Michael and Telsa.

On the Seas

It was January 4, 2012, a misty, damp, wintry morning. England had just recovered from gale-force storms, but the weather didn't matter, I thought; I was going on a Mediterranean cruise.

This was the third consecutive year I had travelled the Mediterranean by ship since Telsa's passing This time though, I was visiting some Eastern European cities that were new to me.

Waiting in Manchester Airport for my flight to Venice to be called, I was looking forward to seeing the sights of Venice once more; it is a beautiful and romantic city.

It was 4 p.m. and I had arrived in Venice, boarded the very large Italian ship and arrived in my cabin. It had a balcony, which was perfect as it meant I could see the wonderful sights from a different angle as we sailed down the Canal Grande past St Mark's Square. We entered the open sea of the Adriatic, from where our next stop was to be Bari, on the eastern side of the heel of the "boot" of Italy.

I retired to bed and tried to open the balcony door, but realized it was impossible as the weather had suddenly changed and we were in stormy seas. I still felt very comfortable and safe in my cosy cabin; I had encountered storms in the Mediterranean before. I fell asleep, not particularly worried and tired after a full day of travelling.

I woke up properly at about 5.30 a.m. after a restless night of tossing and turning. I looked out of my window; it was still dark but I could hear the waves crashing on the side of the huge ship. Daylight slowly began to emerge and I could see just how angry the sea had become. I could hear a lot of movement; the whole ship seemed to be up and about – not surprising really as surely no one could have slept through all that.

At breakfast, the captain announced over the tannoy that we would not be stopping at Bari; its port was closed due to the bad weather. Instead we were going further south to another port.

A few minutes later another announcement was made to say that all ports were closed and, as the weather was getting worse as we neared the Mediterranean, the captain had decided to turn round and go back to Venice. We were all shocked – we had only been at sea for 36 hours – but we remained in good spirits and tried to ignore the rough rocky sea.

I was joined at my table in the restaurant by a lovely young Croatian couple. Luckily they spoke English and we were chatting when all of a sudden the ship lurched right over to 45 degrees and stayed there. Crashing sounds came from the kitchen and the dining tables began to slide to the other end of the ship. We desperately tried to keep hold of the glasses and plates on the table. People were screaming and crying and some were on the floor. It felt as though we had all been thrown into the set of *Titanic*. After about what must have been only a couple of minutes but felt like for ever, the ship slowly began to right itself, only to lurch over again a few minutes later. By this time I was beginning to feel very worried.

Just then I noticed a bright green dog shape sitting on the empty chair beside me. It was Telsa; she had come to help me to stay calm in the eye of the storm. I began calling to the angels, particularly Archangel Michael, to lift the ship upright again. Just as before, the ship slowly started to move upright. I wondered what would happen if it lurched again and tipped over completely; I wasn't a strong swimmer and Telsa couldn't swim when she was incarnate. I quickly tried to put those thoughts out of my head.

Everyone was vacated from the dining room, with traumatized people still crying and screaming, some being carried out and comforted. I stayed where I was, though; even if there was going to be a third lurch I felt safe with Telsa beside me.

The captain seemed to gain control and we began to move at full steam through the stormy waters, heading back to the north. I knew it would take us at least another 36 hours to get back to Venice.

That night I couldn't sleep; the ship made some very strange and alarming noises as it fought to hold its own in the storm. I prayed to the angels for most of the night, asking for strength and courage to deal with this traumatic experience and the possibility of going overboard in the freezing, dark night. Telsa spent most of the night beside me on my bed.

At last dawn started to break. I was exhausted, but we had made it through the night and the ship seemed to be in control as the storm began to subside. Telsa left my side, obviously knowing that I was safe now.

My dearest friend had again come to my aid in my hour of need to comfort me and give me strength and courage.

Eventually we arrived in Ravenna, where many people disembarked, and a few hours later those of us who had stayed were off down the Adriatic Sea once again.

The cruise went ahead, although it was shorter than had been scheduled; we called in at Israel and, briefly, Rhodes and Athens, back once again to Venice and from there home.

I learned later that another cruise ship, the *Costa Concordia*, had run aground on the western side of Italy.

We had had a lot of drama on our ship, but we had all come out of it safely. Tragically, some of the passengers on the *Costa* were not so lucky.

Those of us who completed the cruise became a community, and the rest of the trip was like being on a ship with friends and family.

The events seemed to have made everyone realize what was truly important to them; everyone I spoke to said they had been praying to someone.

How sad that it is often disaster and loss of life, or being close to loss of life, that makes people come together and rethink their lives.

But thank you angels and thank you Telsa, once again, for your presence and healing.

Spiritual Beings of the Unusual Kind

It was July 2012, a beautiful summer's day; I remember it as we had not had many of those days! I had just finished hosting a weekend workshop at my house in Bedale.

After everyone had gone home, I had something to eat, relaxed and later went to bed, feeling pleased with how things had gone over the weekend. I put the light out and almost immediately, there before me as though it had been waiting for me, I saw at the bottom of the bed an emerald-green ant-like being. It was wearing a green uniform and standing very still, facing sideways, so as not to appear confrontational. It seemed to be about the size of a human. At first I was shocked and a bit fearful, but then I realized that Telsa, my faithful friend, had appeared and was sitting up at my right-hand side. Rather bizarrely, she was wearing a pale grey uniform.

She was there to help me to see this being and not be afraid of it. I said to the being that was enough for now, I had seen it and acknowledged its presence but that was enough for me to cope with for the moment. It stayed still for a few more moments, then disappeared. It had been very respectful, I felt, and had left at my request.

I lay back in wonder at what had just happened. Then the whole sky opened up in front of me, a vortex, the same as had happened to me before when I was on Mount Olympus looking at the night sky; on that occasion I had seen lightships whizzing about, entering and exiting our planet.

Now the ceiling and roof seemed to be dissolving and opening up to the night sky. I could see amazingly bright stars and planets. A grey lightship then slowly emerged through my bedroom wall. I knew Telsa was still beside me on my right-hand side and I could tell that she was connected to this lightship and was trying to show me something. The ship hovered in the room for a while and then, slowly and gently, it circled over my head, imprinting me with golden light symbols and light rays.

Usually when Telsa has come to help she has lain on my bed to comfort and heal me, but this was very different. She was sitting up, alert, keeping me calm but overseeing and at the same time: she was doing a job. I was just starting to feel a bit overwhelmed with it all when my father's face appeared to me from spirit, and I felt comforted and that everything was OK.

The ship began to lower down over me and Telsa got into it through a sliding door on its underside. Someone was sliding it closed after her, but I could not see who or what. Then the ship left, very gently but with speed, just as I had seen them in the night sky above Mount Olympus that time.

When the ship had disappeared the sky opened up again above my bedroom, the stars, planets and lines of pale golden light forming a grid above me connecting Earth to the heavens.

When it was over I wrote it all down, so I didn't just think in the morning that it had been a dream. When I looked at my notebook after waking up in the morning I remembered and knew that it had all really happened.

It is wonderful for me to know that Telsa is now doing a lot more than just healing. She is helping and teaching from the spirit world to show me more about the universe and the galactic beings.

All Our Animals
are Healers

The true experiences I have told of in this book will, I hope, be enlightening and help people understand just what our animals are capable of if we only give them a chance.

Many people are unaware of the special qualities that our dogs, cats and other animals bring to our planet. They are such loving, faithful companions to humans if we allow them to be; most pet owners would testify to the unconditional love their pets give them, but also foremost among their qualities is healing.

Animals incarnate onto this planet with their sense of being connected to the Divine intact, while the majority of we humans have forgotten our divinity and have to work our way back to it, through challenging experiences and often, pain. Our animals are trying to teach us by example the ways of kindness, love and oneness with each other

Some animals are treated barbarically, especially in my opinion those that are caged, abused and tortured for experiments and for food. I believe that those animals that offer themselves to us for food deserve at the very least a decent life and a humane and comfortable death.

Pet animals give us so much love and ask for very little in return; just food, a bed for the night and human company.

Our animals also lovingly take on our emotional and physical burdens, even though many of us are not aware of this. Again they do it with unconditional love because they want to help us. They are animal angels.

The laws of the universe state that what we give out we get back, whether in this lifetime or the next. We should think about what we might be creating for ourselves by treating our animals as inferior beings.

In Atlantis humans and animals lived happily together, learning from each other with respect and trust. Many people now are waking up to realize that we can live our lives with love, compassion, harmony and grace; that we can live peacefully together with our animals.

And I am very much aware there are some wonderful people doing wonderful things to help animals that are ill-treated, abused or abandoned.

I have been so privileged to have been made aware of the highly evolved nature of animals while working with my most special dog, Telsa, who only wanted to help heal people and give them all of her unconditional love. She taught me, and many others, many valuable lessons while she was here as my partner.

God bless you Telsa. All my love and thanks for coming into my life and sharing your profound healing gift as my healing partner.

Until we meet again!

TELSA
...from Rosemary

Always busy as a bee
Curiosity flowing free
Observant for both of us
Telepathy without the fuss
Natural healer that's for sure
Always coming back with more
Everyone would sit in our groups
While you always jumped thru hoops
To get the necessary healing done
Didn't need reward of a bone

You enjoyed your life to the full
Romping thru fields without lull
Waiting to see what was round the bend
In case there was a heart to mend

Opening hearts was your thing
Making others' hearts sing
I believe you could fly
I believe you could touch the sky
I would still like to fly with you
Maybe Telsa that's what we can do.

From ME to YOU, TELSA
with love xxx Rosemary

About the Author

Rosemary Stephenson is a Sacred Sound Teacher, Healer and Practitioner. She is the Founder and Teacher of C.R.O.S.S. Crescendo Reiki Of Sacred Sound Healing System. Rosemary has trained with the Diana Cooper School of Angels and Ascension, in Angelic Reiki and Sounds of Ascension, and is a Master Facilitator for Gaiadon Heart.

Rosemary lives just outside the beautiful market town of Bedale in North Yorkshire where she organizes events nationwide, courses and sound healing sessions for groups and individual sessions.

For more information about Rosemary and her work please visit *www.celestiallighthealers.com*

Email: *rosemary@celestiallighthealers.com*

Tel. +44 (0) 7775 854640

Further Findhorn Press Titles

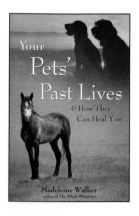

Your Pets Past Lives

by Madeleine Walker

An investigation into animals and past-life healing, this work delves deep into the profound connections between people and their non-human companions.

978-1-84409-572-8

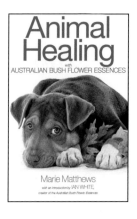

Animal Healing

by Marie Matthews

This comprehensive reference gives extraordinary insights into the emotional world of animals and explores the healing powers of Australian Bush Flower Essences.

978-1-84409-610-7

Bach Flower Remedies For Dogs

by Martin J Scott & Gael Mariani

Using this book, any owner can quickly learn to master this safe and effective system to help the dogs they love with a whole range of problems – from puppyhood to old age.

978-1-84409-099-0